Oriental
CROSS STITCH

Oriental
CROSS STITCH

Debbie Minton

C&B
COLLINS & BROWN

To my Mum, who is always there with love, help and advice.

First published in Great Britain in 1999
by Collins & Brown Ltd
London House
Great Eastern Wharf
Parkgate Road
London SW11 4NQ

135798642
British Library Cataloguing-in-Publications Data:
A catalogue record for this book
is available from the British Library.

ISBN 1 85585 6751 (hardback edition)
ISBN 1 85585 7006 (paperback edition)

Editor: Heather Dewhurst
Designer: Sara Kidd
Photographer: Shona Wood
Reproduction by Hong Kong Graphic and Printing Ltd
Printed and bound in Spain by Graficas Estella
Distributed in the United States and Canada by Sterling Publishing Co,
387 Park Avenue South, New York, NY 10016, USA

Contents

Introduction

Well, I've done it at last – my wonderful Oriental Cross Stitch book! This book has been in my mind and heart for a long time - many of the designs were drawn several years ago - and I am really pleased it is now finally published!

For a long time, I have had a passion for the Orient and collect all sorts of oriental artefacts. Indeed, when I was in the USA a few years ago, I bought so many Japanese books, fans and silk paintings, that I had to buy two large suitcases in which to bring them home!

In my hall at home I have a large watercolour of a beautiful Japanese lady kneeling with a rice bowl in her hands. Her kimono is pale gold and decorated with lilies and lotus flowers. The painting is very peaceful and I find that it gives me an inner calm when I look at it. I find that oriental art and design often produces a tranquil effect. Perhaps this is to do with the colours and elegance of the kimonos, the delicacy and beauty of the flowers or the graceful way in which birds and animals are drawn.

When I was creating the designs for this book, my husband and children would often find me in the dining room, usually on the floor, surrounded by at least a dozen Japanese and Chinese art and design books. After reading through all these books, I developed a 'feel' for the delicate flowers, the poses of the creatures, the colours and designs of kimonos, and even a feel for the hairstyles of oriental ladies. Because I love the subject matter, I find that creating oriental cross stitch designs simply 'happened'.

I hope that, through looking at the designs in this book, some of my enthusiasm for the Orient will rub off on to you and that you will enjoy stitching my designs as much as I have enjoyed designing them.

Crane in Winter

I love the combination of subtle colours in this design. The soft pinks, blues and yellows of the crane's feathers stand out clearly against the snow-covered branch and leaves of the tree to make a delicate cross-stitch composition.

ACTUAL DESIGN SIZE

5½ x 6in (14 x 15cm)

MATERIALS

• 1 piece of 16-count Aida in white measuring approximately 10⅜ x 11in (26 x 27.5cm)
• No 24 tapestry needle

THREADS

DMC Colour		40in (1m) lengths
310	black	3
676	mustard	1
677	pale yellow	1
680	sandy brown	2
762	silver grey	4
776	pink	3
819	pale pink	3
869	khaki	1
890	dark green	3
938	dark brown	1
3753	smoky blue	3

COLOUR FOR BACKSTITCHING

Backstitch all outlines using 310.

INSTRUCTIONS

Mark the centre of the chart. Find the centre of your fabric and make long tacking stitches across and down as guidelines. Using two strands of stranded cotton (except for backstitching where you use one strand only), begin your stitching following the chart. For full instructions for cross stitches, backstitches and special shaping stitches see the *Techniques* section on pages 122-127 of this book.

KEY

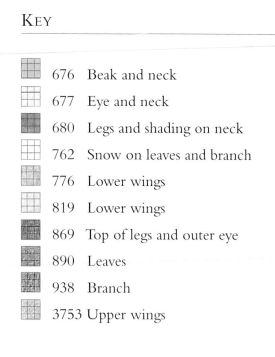 676 Beak and neck

677 Eye and neck

680 Legs and shading on neck

762 Snow on leaves and branch

776 Lower wings

819 Lower wings

869 Top of legs and outer eye

890 Leaves

938 Branch

3753 Upper wings

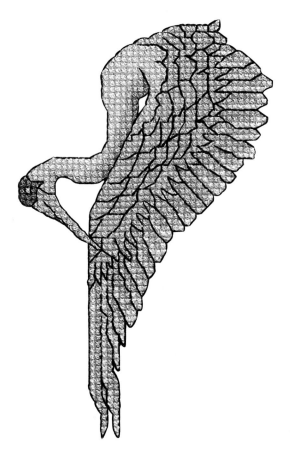

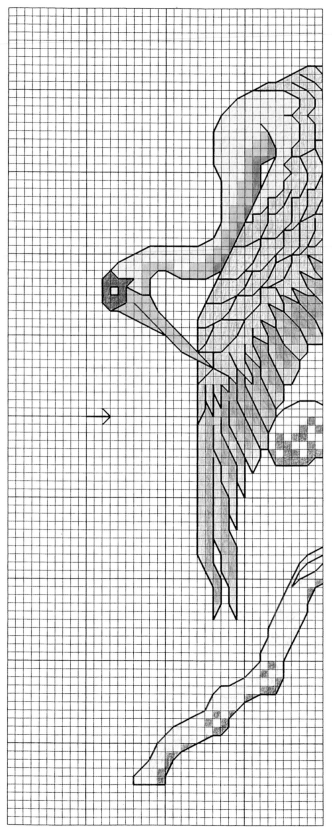

Birds of Paradise

These pretty-coloured birds of paradise are depicted singing to each other through the branches, and they make a lovely embellishment for a lace-trimmed pillow. If you prefer, you could frame the design as a picture, or stitch just one of the birds to decorate the top of a trinket box or make a greetings card.

ACTUAL DESIGN SIZE

9¼ x 7½ in (23 x 19cm)

MATERIALS

• 1 piece of Lawn Cotton in white measuring approximately 13¼ x13¼in (33 x 33cm)
• 1 piece of 14-count waste canvas measuring approximately 11¼ x 9½in (28 x 24cm)
• No 24 tapestry needle
• 1 piece of white backing cloth measuring approximately 13¼ x 13¼in (33 x 33cm)
• 1 white zip measuring 10in (25cm)
• Broderie anglaise measuring approximately 50in (125cm)
• 1 cushion pad measuring 12 x 12in (30 x 30cm)

THREADS

DMC Colour		40in (1m) lengths
310	black	1
469	dark green	1
471	green	1
472	light green	1
796	royal blue	1
799	cornflower blue	1
800	pale blue	1
898	brown	1
951	flesh pink	1
3825	apricot	1

COLOURS FOR BACKSTITCHING

Backstitch the twigs using 898.
Backstitch the beaks using 3825.

FRENCH KNOTS

Birds' eyes use 310.

INSTRUCTIONS

Mark the centre of the chart. Find the centre of your fabric and make long tacking stitches across and down. Place the waste canvas centrally on the fabric and tack into position, leaving a ⅝in (1.5cm) seam all the way around. Oversew or overlock the edges of the lawn cotton. Mark the centre of the waste canvas with tacking stitches. Using two strands of stranded cotton (except for backstitching where you use one strand only), begin your work following the chart. For full instructions for waste canvas, cross stitches, backstitches and French Knots see the *Techniques* section on pages 122-127 of this book.

MAKING THE CUSHION

Turn and press ⅝in (1.5cm) on all sides of the backing cloth and stitched cotton. Tack and stitch the zip tape to one pressed edge of the backing cloth, concealing the teeth. Gather the broderie anglaise evenly to measure 48in (120cm). Match the centre of the lace to the top centre of the worked piece, right sides together, and tack in place around all four sides of the fabric, overlapping the joining edges. Stitch together on the wrong side. Place the right sides of the cushion front and backing cloth together, sandwiching the lace, and machine stitch around three sides to each end of the zip. Tack and stitch the zip to the cushion front. If using pins, check to make sure you have removed them all. Trim the fabric around the corners, then open the zip and turn the cushion cover the right side out. Insert a cushion pad and close the zip to complete.

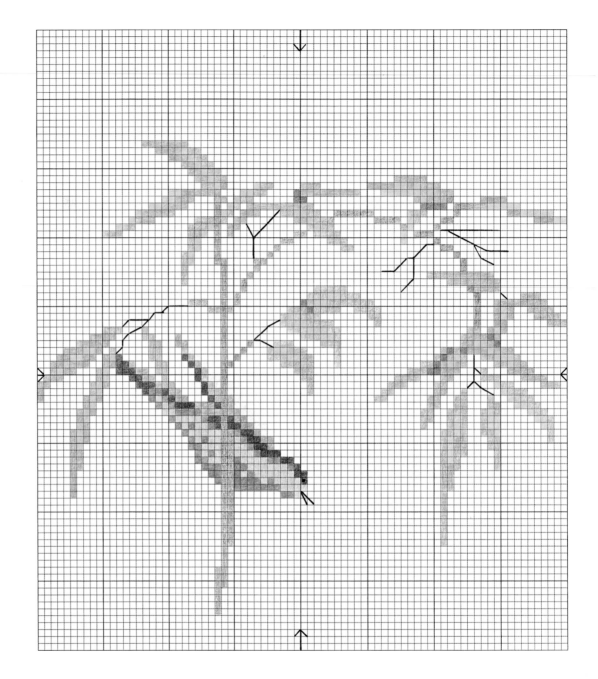

KEY

<table>
<tr><td> 469</td><td>Dark leaves</td><td>799</td><td>Mid-toned feathers</td></tr>
</table>

469	Dark leaves	
471	Mid-toned leaves	
472	Pale leaves	
796	Dark feathers	

799	Mid-toned feathers
800	Pale feathers
898	Branch
951	Breasts and heads
3825	Breasts and heads

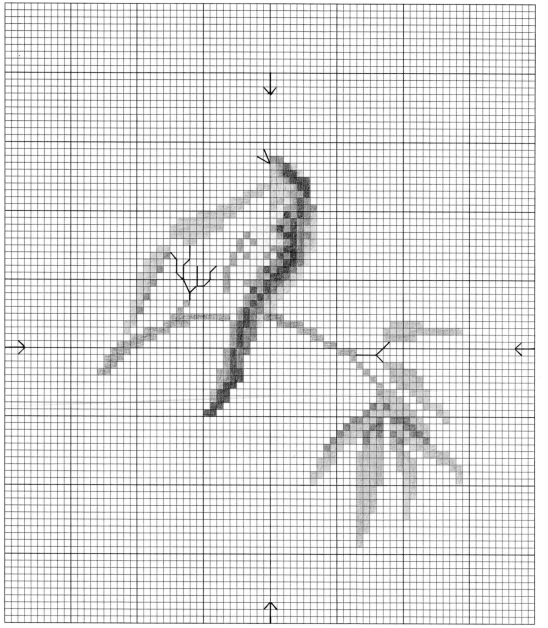

Oriental Bird

I designed this diminutive bird of paradise perched on a branch to add a touch of elegance to a small silver-framed trinket box. You could also mount the design in a circular framed gift card.

ACTUAL DESIGN SIZE

3 x 3in (7.5 x 7.5cm)

MATERIALS

• 1 piece of 16-count Aida in cream measuring approximately 8 x 8in (20 x 20cm)
• No 24 tapestry needle
• Trinket box (optional)

THREADS

DMC Colour		40in (1m) lengths
310	black	1
319	dark green	1
320	green	1
644	grey	1
725	yellow	1
796	royal blue	1
798	blue	1
809	light blue	1
898	dark brown	1
3326	pale pink	1
3328	dark pink	1
3753	smoky blue	1

COLOURS FOR BACKSTITCHING

Backstitch front and bottom of black head piece using 310.
Backstitch leaves using 319.

Backstitch feet using 644.
Backstitch eye using 725.
Backstitch wings, tail and back using 796.
Backstitch contrasting stitching on head crest using 798.
Backstitch right side of body next to tail using 3326.
Backstitch flowers and bottom edge of body using 3328.
Backstitch head crest using 3753.

FRENCH KNOTS

Bird's eye use 310.

INSTRUCTIONS

Mark the centre of the chart. Find the centre of your fabric and make long tacking stitches across and down. Using two strands of stranded cotton (except for backstitching where you use one strand only), begin your work following the chart. For full instructions for cross stitches, backstitches, special shaping stitches and French Knots see the *Techniques* section on pages 122-127 of this book. Make up the trinket box following the manufacturer's instructions.

KEY

310 Head piece

319 Dark leaves

320 Mid-toned leaves

644 Feet

796 Dark areas of tail and wings

798 Mid-toned areas of head crest, tail and wings

809 Light areas of head crest, tail and wings

898 Branch

3326 Flower centres and pale area of breast

3328 Flower petals, beak and dark area of breast

3753 Head crest

This pretty bird is watching warily from his safe perch.

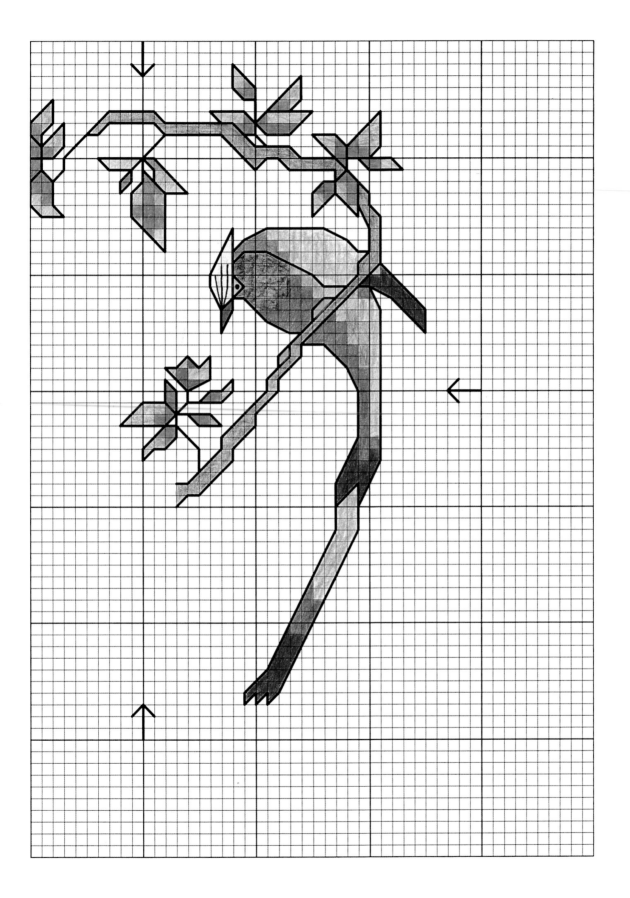

Chinese Dragon

No book on oriental design would be complete without a Chinese dragon, and this stunning cushion features a resplendent fiery red and gold dragon complete with bared fangs and claws. This cross-stitch design is sure to become a talking point in whichever room it is displayed.

ACTUAL DESIGN SIZE

9½ x 9in (24 x 22.5cm)

MATERIALS

• 1 piece of 18-count Aida in black measuring approximately 18 x 18in (45 x 45cm)
• No 24 tapestry needle
• Black cotton measuring approximately 16 x 16in (40 x 40cm)
• 1 black zip measuring 9in (22.5cm)
• Gold and black cord measuring approximately 50in (125cm)
• 1 cushion pad measuring 12 x 12in (30 x 30cm)

THREADS

DMC Colour		40in (1m) lengths
310	black	8
666	red	21
725	yellow	16
White		2
D282 metallic gold		3

COLOUR FOR BACKSTITCHING

Backstitch all outlines using 310.

INSTRUCTIONS

Mark the centre of the chart. Find the centre of your fabric and make long tacking stitches across and down. Using two strands of stranded cotton (except for backstitching where you use one strand only), begin your work following the chart. For full instructions for cross stitches, backstitches, special shaping stitches and long stitches see the *Techniques* section on pages 122-127 of this book.

MAKING THE CUSHION

Trim the Aida fabric to approximately 16in (40cm) square, then trim the backing cloth to the same size. Turn over ⅝in (1.5cm) on one edge of the backing fabric and press. Tack and stitch the zip tape to the pressed edge, concealing the teeth. If using pins, count the number of pins as you use them and count them again when you have removed them to make sure there are no pins left in your cushion cover. Place the right sides of the cushion front and backing cloth together and machine stitch around three sides, leaving the bottom zipped edge unstitched. Tack and stitch the zip to the cushion front, inserting a small piece of leftover Aida at one end to make a loop. Leave an opening at each end of the zip. Trim the fabric

around the corners, them open the zip and turn the cushion the right side out. Slipstitch the opening at one end of the zip.

Twist the gold and the black cord together and insert one end into the loop and secure with a few small stitches. Slipstitch the cord around the sides of cover while gently twisting it. When you reach the beginning, insert the end into the loop and secure with a few small stitches.

Slipstitch this opening closed. Insert a cushion pad and zip up the cover to complete.

KEY

 D282 Centre of paws, ears, beard and tail and claw highlights

310 Nostrils and eye pupils

666 Body

725 Outer edges of body, horns, facial features and paws

White Teeth, claws, ears and whites of eyes

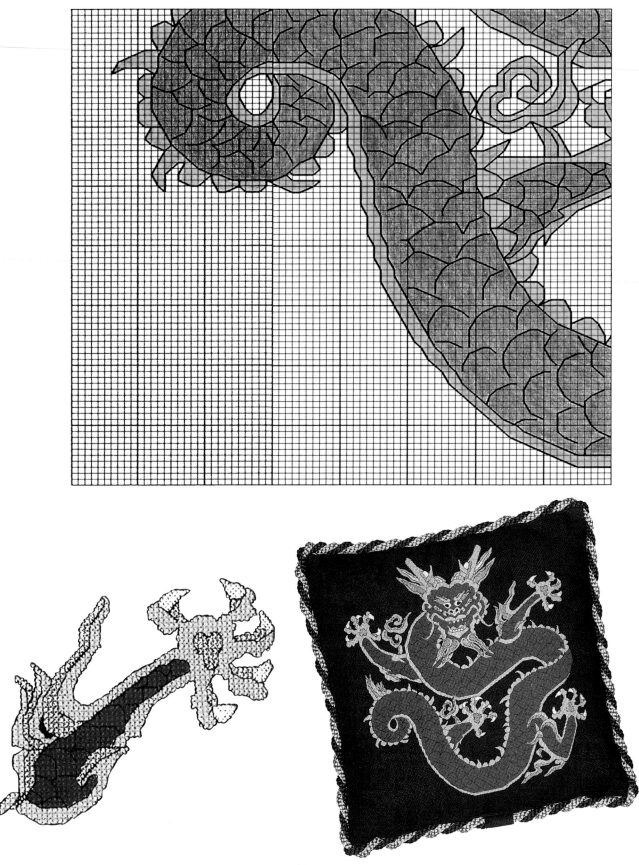

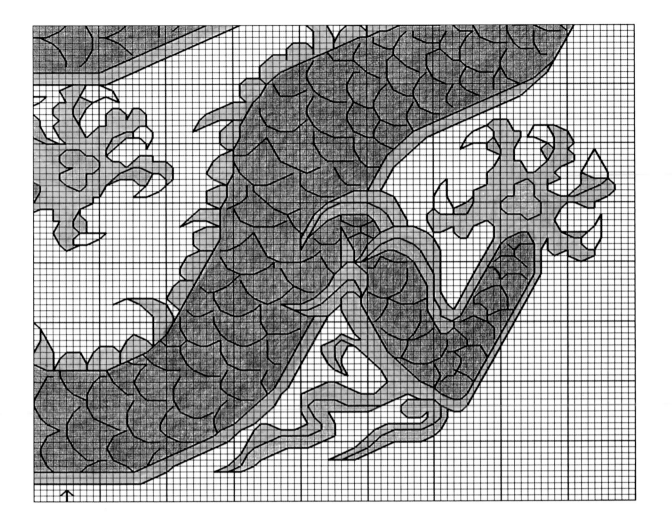

page 22	page 23
page 24	page 25

This diagram shows the position of the four charts that make up this design. You can find the central starting point of the design by following the 'across' and 'down' arrows shown on the portion of the chart on page 23.

Jumping Koi

I love to watch koi gliding through the water, their bright coloured scales glistening in the sunlight. This picture emphasizes the beautiful, rich colours of these fish which are prized so highly in Japan. I designed this koi jumping out of the water to add vitality and movement to the piece.

ACTUAL DESIGN SIZE

5³⁄₈x 7¼in (13.5 x 18cm)

MATERIALS

• 1 piece of 16-count Aida in black measuring approximately 10⅜ x 12in (26 x 30cm)
• No 24 tapestry needle

THREADS

DMC Colour	40in (1m) lengths
310 black	2
740 bright orange	3
741 light orange	3
742 apricot	3
743 bright yellow	4
745 straw yellow	4
799 cornflower blue	8
820 royal blue	1
900 brick	1
918 dark terracotta	1
919 terracotta	1
947 orange	1

COLOURS FOR BACKSTITCHING

Backstitch water using 820.
Backstitch koi using 310.

LONG STITCHES

Markings on fins and tail use 310.

INSTRUCTIONS

Mark the centre of the chart. Find the centre of your fabric and make long tacking stitches across and down. Using two strands of stranded cotton (except for backstitching where you use one strand only), begin your work following the chart. For full instructions for cross stitches, backstitches, special shaping stitches and long stitches see the *Techniques* section on pages 122-127 of this book.

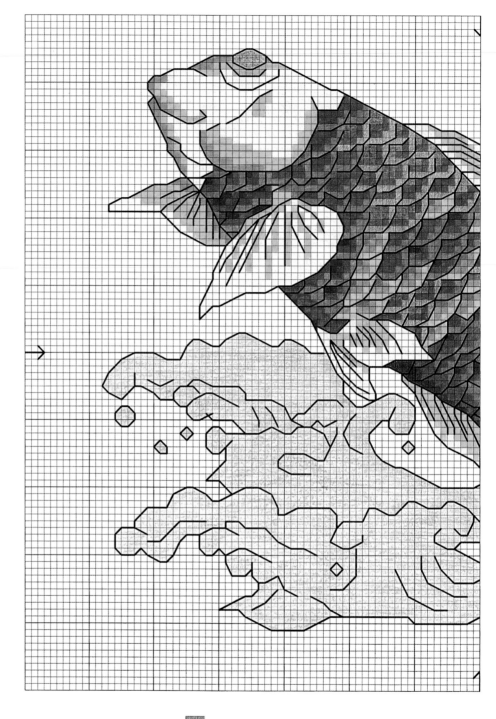

KEY

 310 Eye

740 Centre of orange scales

741 Outer edge of orange scales

742 Light scales, head, fins and tail

743 Light scales, head, fins and tail

745 Head, fins and tail main colour

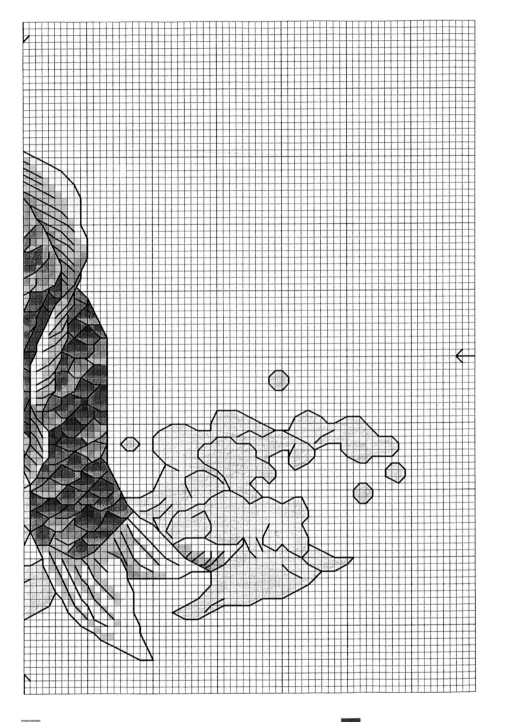

799 Water

900 Outer edge of dark scales

918 Dark scales

919 Inner edge of dark scales

947 Scales and lower edge of koi

The Cricket

This charming design of a cricket resting on a branch is quick to stitch because of its size and simplicity. You could use this design to decorate a place mat or pillow slip using waste canvas, or frame it as shown to make a delightful picture for your wall.

ACTUAL DESIGN SIZE

3¾ x 7½in (9.5 x 19cm)

MATERIALS

- 1 piece of 16-count Aida in white measuring approximately 8¼ x 12½in (21.5 x 31.5cm)
- No 24 tapestry needle

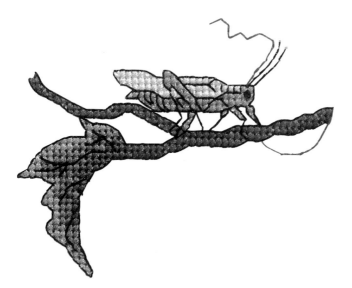

THREADS

DMC Colour	40in (1m) lengths
310 black	1
433 brown	1
677 fawn	1
726 dark yellow	1
727 yellow	1
733 ochre	1
898 dark brown	1
919 terracotta	1
986 dark green	1
987 green	2
989 light green	3
3078 lemon yellow	1

COLOURS FOR BACKSTITCHING

Backstitch entwining twig around branch using 919.
Backstitch all other outlines using 310.

LONG STITCHES

Cricket's antennae use 310.

FRENCH KNOTS

Cricket's eye use 310.

INSTRUCTIONS

Mark the centre of the chart. Find the centre of
your fabric and make long tacking stitches
across and down. Using two strands of stranded
cotton (except for backstitching where you use
one strand only), begin your work following the
chart. For full instructions for cross stitches,
backstitches, special shaping stitches, French
Knots and long stitches see the *Techniques*
section on pages 122–127 of this book.

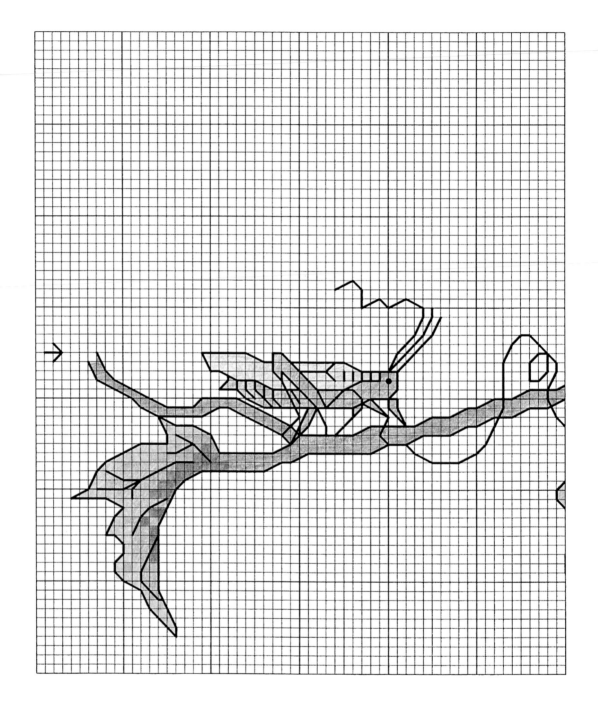

KEY

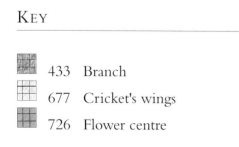

433 Branch

677 Cricket's wings

726 Flower centre

727 Petals

733 Cricket's lower body

898 Dark shading on branch

986 Dark shading on leaves

987 Mid-toned areas on leaves

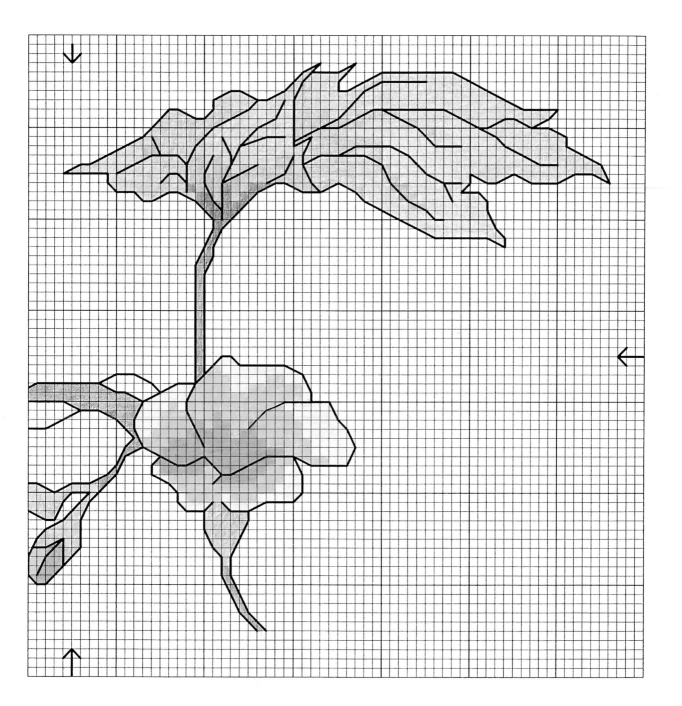

989   Light areas on leaves

3078 Edges of petals

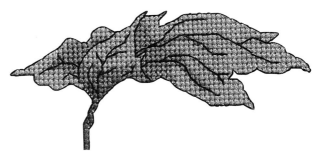

Butterfly and Peony

The delicate unfurling petals of the peony bloom provide an enticing landing place for this beautifully coloured butterfly. This design looks pretty in a gold-rimmed trinket box, but you could mount it in a small gold frame or use it to decorate a small pillow if you prefer.

ACTUAL DESIGN SIZE

2¾ x 3in (7 x 7.5cm)

MATERIALS

• 1 piece of 32-count Linen in ivory approximately 5 x 5in (12.5 x 12.5cm)
• No 24 tapestry needle
• Trinket box (optional)

THREADS

DMC Colour		40in (1m) lengths
613	pale khaki	1
726	yellow	1
801	dark brown	1
869	brown	1
959	mint green	1
986	dark green	1
988	green	1
989	light green	1
995	blue	1
3078	pale yellow	1
3705	dark pink	1
3706	pink	1

COLOURS FOR BACKSTITCHING

Backstitch leaves and veins using 986.

Backstitch flowers using 3705.
Backstitch butterfly wings using 995.
Backstitch butterfly body and twig using 801.

LONG STITCHES

Markings on butterfly wings and antennae use 801.

INSTRUCTIONS

Mark the centre of the chart. Find the centre of your fabric and make long tacking stitches across and down. Using two strands of stranded cotton (except for backstitching where you use one strand only), begin your work following the chart. For full instructions for cross stitches, backstitches, special shaping stitches and long stitches see the *Techniques* section on pages 122-127 of this book. Make up the trinket box following the manufacturer's instructions.

KEY

- 613 Butterfly body
- 726 Inner butterfly wing
- 801 Dark shading on main stem
- 869 Flower stems
- 959 Centre of butterfly wings
- 986 Outer edge of leaves
- 988 Mid-green area of leaves
- 989 Inner leaf area
- 995 Outer edge of butterfly wings
- 3078 Outer edge of petals
- 3705 Centre of flowers
- 3706 Mid-pink area of flowers

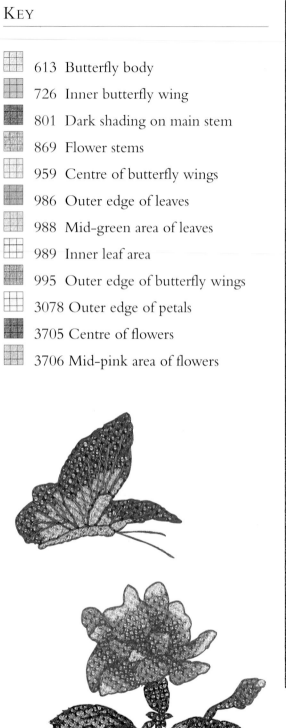

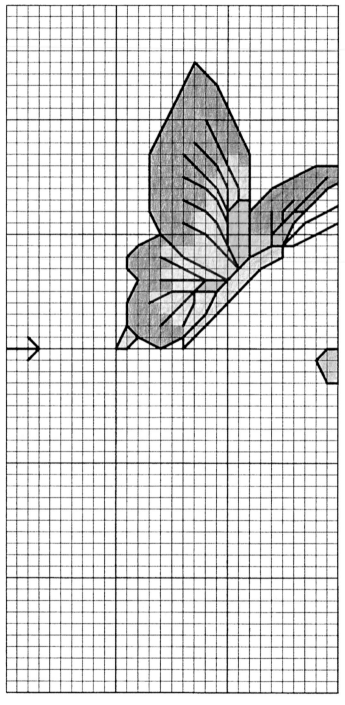

Midnight Kimono

Cranes are important motifs in Japanese art and are used extensively on textiles. The soaring crane featured on this kimono picture is set against a background scene stitched in black, gold and red to make a dramatic piece of art. I stitched this on 36-count linen but you can use 18-count Aida – the finished stitching will be the same size.

ACTUAL DESIGN SIZE

9 x 8½in (22.5 x 21.5cm)

MATERIALS

• 1 piece of 36-count Linen (or 18-count Aida) in ivory measuring approximately 14 x 13½in (35 x 34cm)
• No 24 tapestry needle

THREADS

DMC Colour	40in (1m) lengths
304 claret	2
310 black	46
400 brown	2
581 sage green	2
666 red	3
676 straw	4
677 yellow	2
746 cream	6
958 mint green	2
3706 pink	2
3801 dark pink	2
3812 dark mint green	2
3819 light sage green	3
D282 metallic gold	14

COLOURS FOR BACKSTITCHING

Backstitch semi-circles, scale shapes, clouds and collar using D282.
Backstitch flowers using 304.
Backstitch all other outlines using 310.

INSTRUCTIONS

Mark the centre of the chart. Find the centre of your fabric and make long tacking stitches across and down for guidelines. Using two strands of stranded cotton (except for backstitching where you use one strand only), begin your work following the chart. For full instructions for cross stitches, backstitches and special shaping stitches see the *Techniques* section on pages 122-127 of this book.

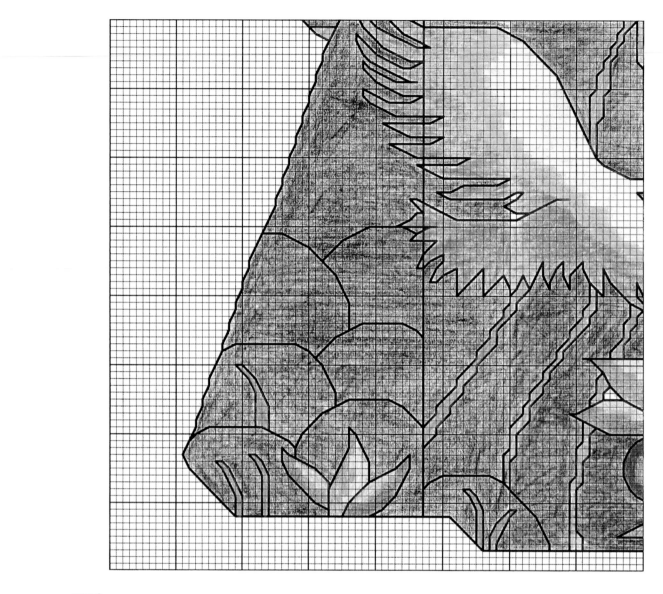

page 40	page 41
page 42	page 43

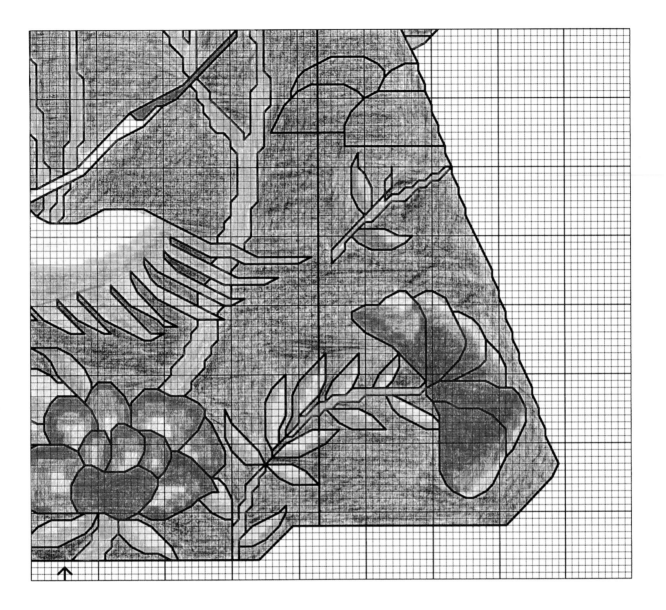

The charts for the Midnight Kimono are on four pages. You will find the central starting point by following the 'across' and 'down' arrows shown on the chart on page 41. Page 40 shows the top left portion of the chart, page 41 the top right, page 42 the bottom left and page 43 the bottom right.

Oriental Portraits

This set of four portraits features different views of Japanese women in traditional dress. The decorative hair ornaments, made from silver, tortoiseshell, coral and jade, draw attention to the beautiful hairstyles favoured by oriental women. You can stitch these pictures as a set, or simply choose your favourite.

SCARLET AND PEACH

ACTUAL DESIGN SIZE

6 x 6in (15 x 15cm)

MATERIALS

• 1 piece of 16-count Aida in cream measuring approximately 11¼ x 11¼in (28 x 28cm)
• No 24 tapestry needle

THREADS

DMC Colour	40in (1m) lengths
310 black	5
349 red	1
351 deep pink	2
352 pink	2
353 pale pink	1
470 green	1
472 pale green	2
712 cream	2
734 olive green	2
834 gold	2
3821 mustard	1
3823 dark cream	1

COLOURS FOR BACKSTITCHING

Backstitch the flower stems around the bamboo frame using 470.
Backstitch all other outlines using 310.

LONG STITCHES

Prongs on hair combs use 3821.

INSTRUCTIONS

Mark the centre of the chart. Find the centre of your fabric and make long tacking stitches across and down. Using two strands of stranded cotton (except for backstitching where you use one strand only), begin your work following the chart. For full instructions for cross stitches, backstitches, special shaping stitches and long stitches see the *Techniques* section on pages 122-127 of this book.

KEY

310 Hair

349 Inner collar and hair bow

351 Flowers

352 Kimono

353 Kimono collar

472/734 Bamboo frame (use 1 strand of each colour)

712 Face and neck

834 Hairpins

3821 Hair combs

3823 Bows on kimono collar

CHERRY RED AND BLUE

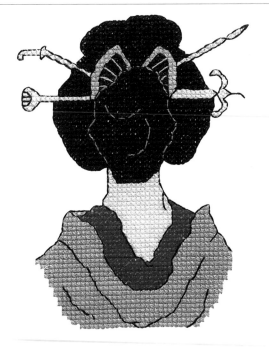

ACTUAL DESIGN SIZE

6 x 6in (15 x 15cm)

MATERIALS

• 1 piece of 16-count Aida in cream measuring approximately 11¼ x 11¼in (28 x 28cm)
• No 24 tapestry needle

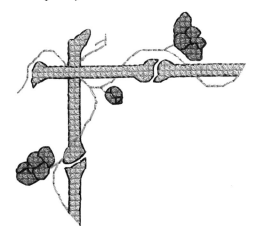

THREADS

DMC Colour	40in (1m) lengths
310 black	5
349 red	1
351 dusky pink	2
470 green	1
472 pale green	1
712 cream	1
734 olive green	1
3755 blue	2
3821 mustard	1
3823 pale yellow	1

COLOURS FOR BACKSTITCHING

Backstitch the flower stems around the bamboo frame using 470.
Backstitch all other outlines using 310.

LONG STITCHES

Prongs on hair combs use 3821.

INSTRUCTIONS

Mark the centre of the chart. Find the centre of your fabric and make long tacking stitches across and down. Using two strands of stranded cotton (except for backstitching where you use one strand only), begin your work following the chart. For full instructions for cross stitches, backstitches, special shaping stitches and long stitches see the *Techniques* section on pages 122-127 of this book.

VIOLET AND BLUE

ACTUAL DESIGN SIZE

6 x 6in (15 x 15cm)

MATERIALS

• 1 piece of 16-count Aida in cream measuring approximately 11¼ x 11¼in (28 x 28cm)
• No 24 tapestry needle

THREADS

DMC Colour	40in (1m) lengths
208 dark purple	2
209 purple	1
310 black	4
334 blue	1
351 pink	2
470 green	1
472 light green	2
712 cream	1
734 olive green	2
3325 light blue	1
3821 mustard	1

COLOURS FOR BACKSTITCHING

Backstitch the flower stems around the bamboo frame using 470.
Backstitch all other outlines using 310.

INSTRUCTIONS

Mark the centre of the chart. Find the centre of your fabric and make long tacking stitches across and down. Using two strands of stranded cotton (except for backstitching where you use one strand only), begin your work following the chart. For full instructions for cross stitches, backstitches and special shaping stitches see the *Techniques* section on pages 122–127 of this book.

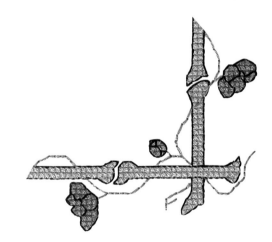

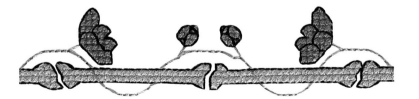

KEY

208 Shading on collar and hair bow

209 Collar and hair bow

310 Hair

334 Shading on kimono and hair decoration

351 Flowers

472/734 Bamboo frame (use 1 strand of each colour)

712 Face

3325 Kimono and hair decoration

3821 Hairpins

LEMON AND LIME

ACTUAL DESIGN SIZE

6 x 6in (15 x 15cm)

MATERIALS

• 1 piece of 16-count Aida in cream measuring approximately 11¼ x 11¼in (28 x 28cm)
• No 24 tapestry needle

THREADS

DMC Colour	40in (1m) lengths
310 black	2
351 deep pink	2
469 dark green	1
470 green	2
471 medium green	2
472 light green	4
676 beige	1
712 cream	2
734 olive green	2
3821 mustard	1
3823 pale yellow	1

COLOURS FOR BACKSTITCHING

Backstitch the flower stems around the bamboo frame using 470.
Backstitch the prongs of the hair combs using 3821.
Backstitch all other outlines using 310.

INSTRUCTIONS

Mark the centre of the chart. Find the centre of your fabric and make long tacking stitches across and down for guidelines. Using two strands of stranded cotton (except for backstitching where you use one strand only), begin your work following the chart. For full instructions for cross stitches, backstitches and special shaping stitches see the *Techniques* section on pages 122-127 of this book.

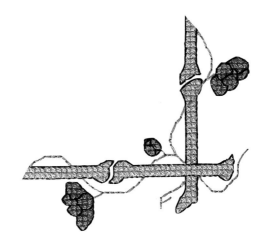

KEY

▩	310 Hair
▩	351 Flowers
▩	469 Dark collar of kimono
▩	471 Inner collar of kimono

▩	472/734 Bamboo frame (use 1 of each colour)
▩	472 Kimono
▩	712 Face and neck
▩	676 Pale collar of kimono
▩	3821 Hair combs
▩	3823 Hairpins

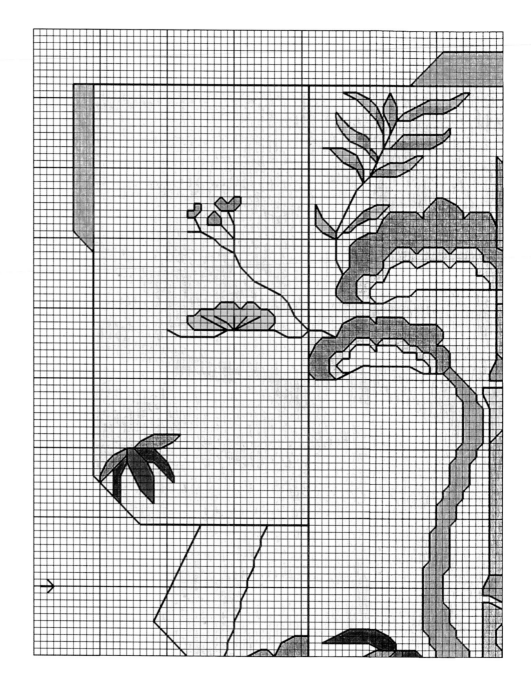

KEY

321	Leaves
349	Thin bamboo stem
400	Soil and small lower twig
581	Leaves
632	Thick bamboo stem
712	Pale area of clouds
721	Leaves and flowers
726	Flowers
747	Background
820	Leaves, and river, bottom right

922 Lower parts of each thick bamboo segment

964 Pale leaves, collar, cuffs and hem of kimono

995 Berries and dark area of clouds

996 Central area of clouds

3770 Top parts of each thick bamboo segment

3776 Light areas of soil

3819 Leaves

D282 Curving central stem

page 58	page 59
page 60	page 61

The charts for the Cool Blue Kimono are split over four pages. You will find the central starting point following the 'across' and 'down' arrows shown on the chart on page 59. Page 58 shows the top left portion of the chart, page 59 the top right, page 60 the bottom left and page 61 the bottom right.

Japanese Empress

I call this tiny stitched lady the 'Japanese Empress' as she looks so petite and regal in her traditional robes. This design was made into a decorative greetings card, but would look equally beautiful framed as a picture.

ACTUAL DESIGN SIZE

3 x 1¼in (7.5 x 3cm)

MATERIALS

• 1 piece of 36-count Linen in ivory measuring approximately 8 x 6¼in (20 x 15.5cm)
• No 24 tapestry needle
• Oval greetings card mount

THREADS

DMC Colour	40in (1m) lengths
Ecru	1
D282 light gold	1
310 black	1
720 tan	1
721 dull orange	1
722 orange	1
945 peach	1
959 mint green	1
3770 pale peach	1
3825 apricot	1

COLOUR FOR BACKSTITCHING

Backstitch all outlines using 310.

LONG STITCHES

Hairpins use gold.

INSTRUCTIONS

Mark the centre of the chart. Find the centre of your fabric and make long tacking stitches across and down. Using two strands of stranded cotton (except for backstitching where you use one strand only), begin your work following the chart. For full instructions for cross stitches, backstitches, special shaping stitches and long stitches see the *Techniques* section on pages 122-127 of this book. Mount the finished piece in an oval greetings card following the instructions in the *Techniques* section.

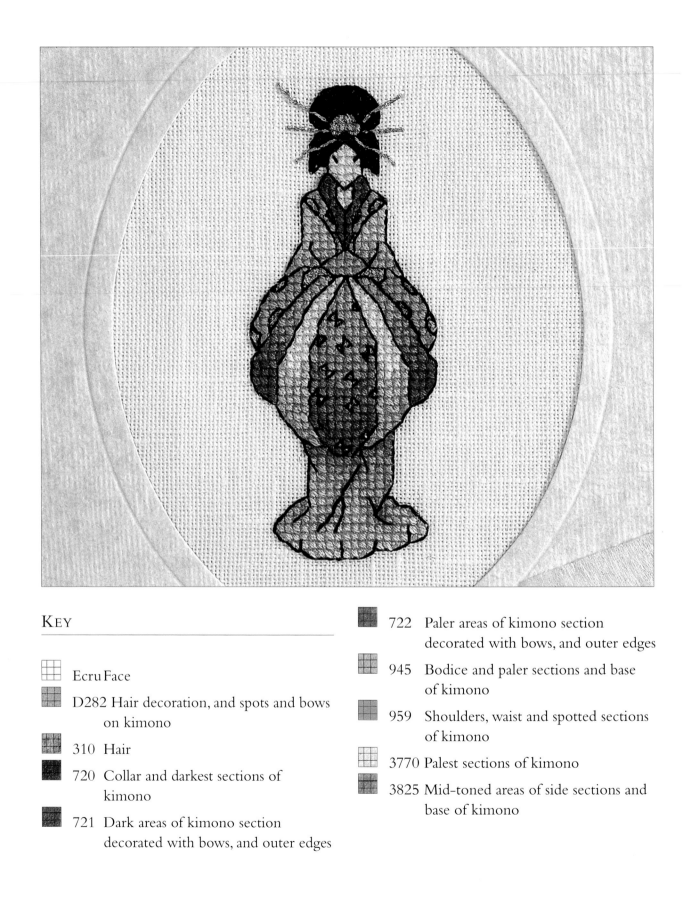

KEY

⊞ Ecru Face

▦ D282 Hair decoration, and spots and bows on kimono

▦ 310 Hair

■ 720 Collar and darkest sections of kimono

▦ 721 Dark areas of kimono section decorated with bows, and outer edges

▦ 722 Paler areas of kimono section decorated with bows, and outer edges

▦ 945 Bodice and paler sections and base of kimono

▦ 959 Shoulders, waist and spotted sections of kimono

⊞ 3770 Palest sections of kimono

▦ 3825 Mid-toned areas of side sections and base of kimono

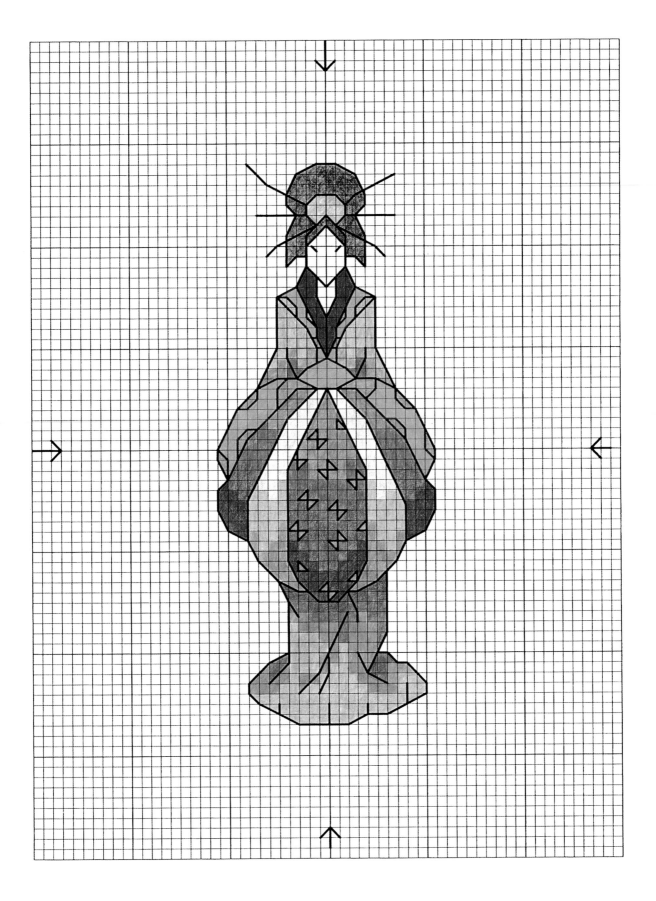

KEY

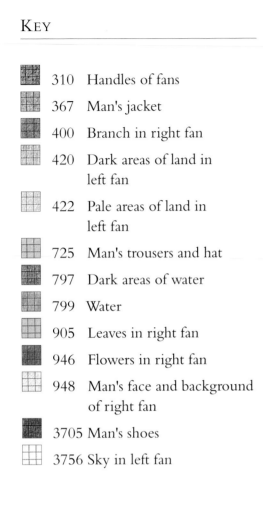

310 Handles of fans

367 Man's jacket

400 Branch in right fan

420 Dark areas of land in left fan

422 Pale areas of land in left fan

725 Man's trousers and hat

797 Dark areas of water

799 Water

905 Leaves in right fan

946 Flowers in right fan

948 Man's face and background of right fan

3705 Man's shoes

3756 Sky in left fan

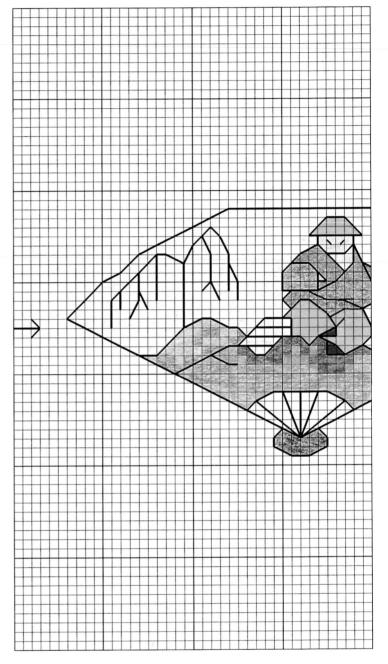

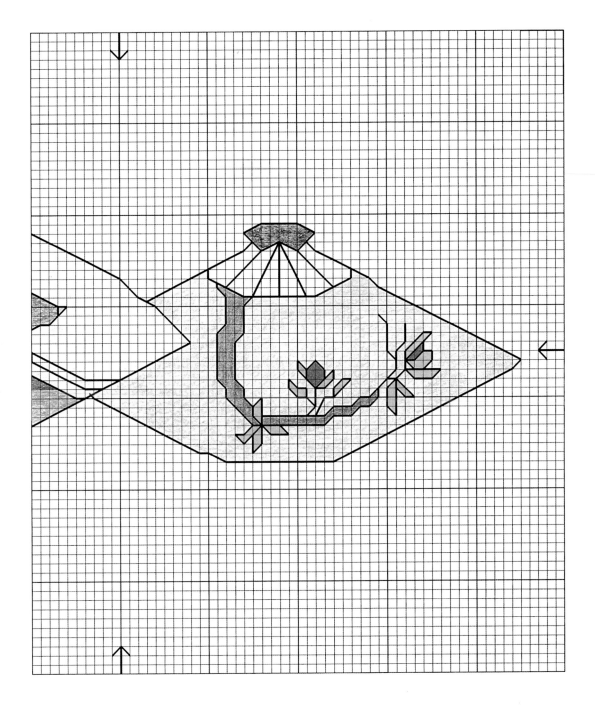

Perfect Serenity

This striking but simple design of flowers on an opened fan was inspired by a recent visit to America when I bought a handful of Japanese display fans featuring a variety of exquisite oriental designs. This design has a serene and timeless quality and would make a stunning centrepiece on a wall.

ACTUAL DESIGN SIZE

7 x 14in (17.5 x 35cm)

MATERIALS

• 1 piece of 18-count Aida in cream measuring approximately 9 x 16in (22.5 x 40cm)
• No 24 tapestry needle

THREADS

DMC Colour	40in (1m) lengths
310 black	4
349 dull red	1
350 red	2
352 pink	8
353 pale pink	3
725 yellow	1
742 orange	1
746 cream	58
898 chocolate brown	1
938 dark brown	1
986 dark green	1
987 green	3
989 light green	2
995 blue	1
3812 jade green	1

COLOURS FOR BACKSTITCHING

Backstitch the fan outline and struts using 310.
Backstitch the petals using 349.
Backstitch the leaves using 986.
Backstitch the flower stems, and dragonfly's tail and antennae using 938.
Backstitch the lettering using two strands of 310.

LONG STITCHES

Flower stamens use 742.

FRENCH KNOTS

Flower buds use 349.

INSTRUCTIONS

Mark the centre of the chart. Find the centre of your fabric and make long tacking stitches across and down. Using two strands of stranded cotton (except for backstitching where you use one strand only), begin your work following the chart. For full instructions for cross stitches, backstitches, special shaping stitches, long stitches and French Knots see the *Techniques* section on pages 122–127 of this book.

KEY

310	Fan sticks	
350	Dark parts of flower centres	
352	Mid-toned areas of petals	
353	Pale areas of petals	

725	Flower centres	
746	Background of fan	
898	Dragonfly's body	
938	Flower stems	
986	Dark areas of leaves	
987	Mid-toned areas of leaves	

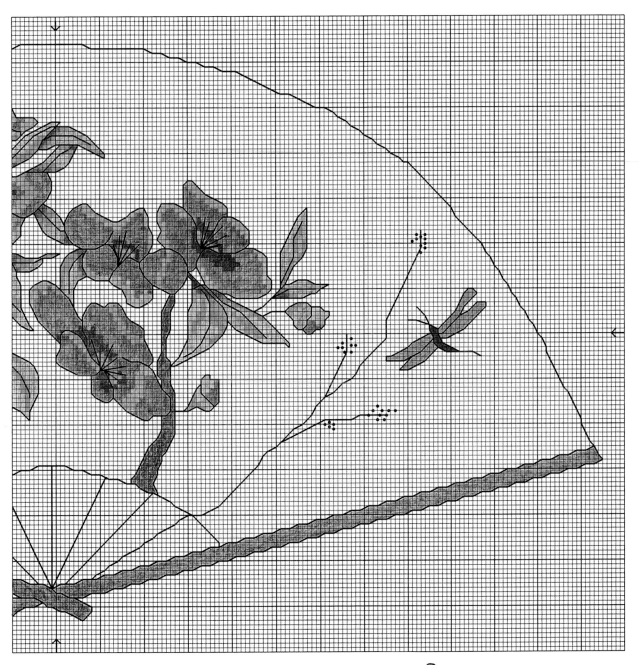

989 Pale areas of leaves

995/3812 Dragonfly's wings (use 1 strand
of each colour)

Pure Tranquillity

This picture of an oriental lady wearing a richly coloured silk kimono and elegantly holding a parasol instantly captures the eastern spirit of tranquillity. The flowers surrounding the figure are suggestive of a fragrant and beautiful spring garden. This is a picture to relax you and deserves pride of place in a restful living room.

ACTUAL DESIGN SIZE

12 x 7½in (30 x 19cm)

MATERIALS

• 1 piece of 16-count Aida in cream measuring approximately 16¾ x 12in (42 x 30cm)
• No 24 tapestry needle

THREADS

DMC Colour	40in (1m) lengths
300 chestnut brown	2
310 black	3
435 brown	3
437 light brown	2
470 dark green	3
472 light green	3
606 red	2
676 straw	2
677 pale straw	4
712 cream	3
739 dark cream	1
741 orange	2
742 yellow	2
743 dark yellow	3
744 pale yellow	3
782 mustard	2
959 mint green	2
963 pale pink	3
964 pale mint green	2
995 bright blue	4
996 blue	3
3340 dark peach	3
3341 peach	4
3705 crimson	5
3706 light crimson	4
3708 pink	2
3824 light peach	3

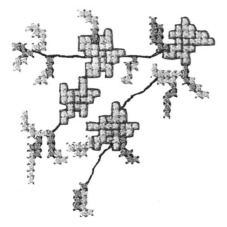

COLOURS FOR BACKSTITCHING

Backstitch the blossom using 3705.
Backstitch the branches using 300.
Backstitch the lips using 606.
Backstitch the leaf and flower stems on the kimono using 470.
Backstitch the eyes and eyebrows using 310.
Backstitch the spokes on the parasol using 435.

LONG STITCHES

Hairpins use 300.

FRENCH KNOTS

Eyes of fish on kimono use 310.

INSTRUCTIONS

Mark the centre of the chart. Find the centre of your fabric and make long tacking stitches across and down. These will act as your guidelines when stitching. Using two strands of stranded cotton (except for backstitching when you use one strand only), begin your work following the chart. For full instructions for cross stitches, backstitches, special shaping stitches, long stitches and French Knots see the *Techniques* section on pages 122-127 of this book.

KEY

	310	Hair
	435	Tip and handle of parasol
	437	Centre spokes on parasol
	470	Dark leaves on dress and blossom
	472	Pale leaves on dress and blossom and hair ornament
	606	Circle decoration on kimono
	676	Lower part of parasol
	677	Underneath of parasol
	712	Face, hand, oval decoration on centre of kimono and pattern on parasol
	739	Shading on neck
	741	Fish on kimono
	742	Fish on kimono and kimono bustle
	743	Hair ornament, kimono bustle and top of parasol
	744	Blossom centres and base of kimono
	782	Circle decoration on kimono and dots at base of kimono
	959	Inner robe
	963	Blossom and hair decoration
	964	Pale areas surrounding fish
	995	Circle decoration on kimono and dark areas surrounding fish
	996	Mid-toned areas surrounding fish and pattern on parasol
	3340	Bodice and centre of kimono
	3341	Bodice and centre of kimono
	3705	Dark areas of collar and at front of kimono, and pattern on parasol
	3706	Pale areas of collar and dark areas at front of kimono
	3708	Dark parts of blossom and decoration on bodice
	3824	Sleeve and centre of kimono

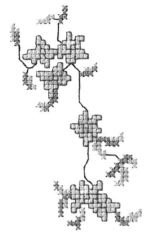

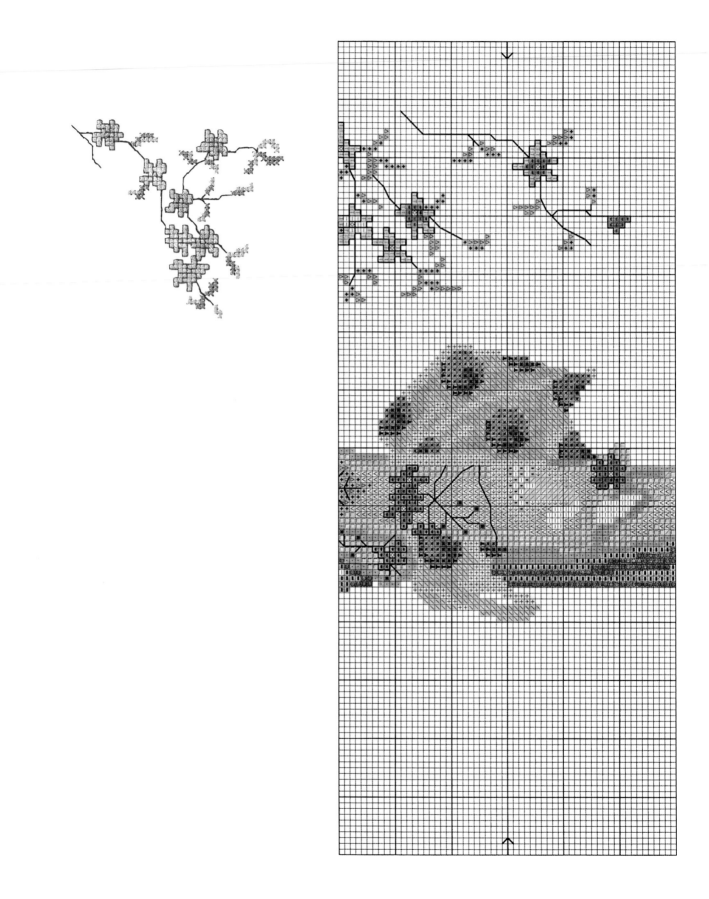

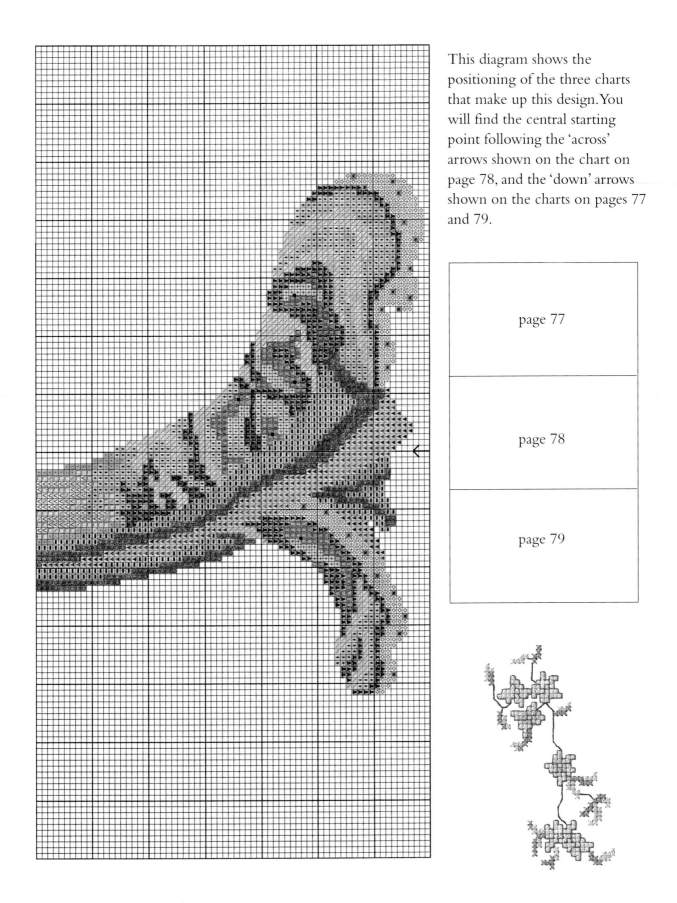

This diagram shows the positioning of the three charts that make up this design. You will find the central starting point following the 'across' arrows shown on the chart on page 78, and the 'down' arrows shown on the charts on pages 77 and 79.

page 77
page 78
page 79

Scarlet Poppies

I love the colour of poppies, especially when there is a huge expanse of scarlet in a poppy field. For this design, I chose to depict two unfurling poppies, framed by a simple blue and yellow border, to decorate a charming herb pillow. As the colour of poppies is so intense, the design was stitched on a khaki background, but you can substitute another colour of Aida if you prefer.

ACTUAL DESIGN SIZE

5¾ x 5¾in (14.5 x 14.5cm)

MATERIALS

• 1 piece of 16-count Aida in khaki measuring approximately 10¾ x 10¾in (27 x 27cm)
• No 24 tapestry needle
• 1 piece of navy cotton measuring approximately 8¼ x 8¼in (21 x 21cm)
• Polyester filling
• Dried herbs

THREADS

DMC Colour	40in (1m) lengths
310 black	2
321 scarlet	1
336 dark blue	8
666 red	1
890 dark green	1
986 green	1
988 light green	1
3705 dark pink	2
3821 mustard	2

COLOURS FOR BACKSTITCHING

Backstitch the frame and the poppy leaves and petals using 310.
Backstitch the gold trellis work in the frame using 3821.

LONG STITCHES

Centre and stamens of poppy use 310.

INSTRUCTIONS

Mark the centre of the chart. Find the centre of your fabric and make long tacking stitches across and down for guidelines. Using two strands of stranded cotton (except for backstitching where you use one strand only), begin your work following the chart. For full instructions for cross stitches, backstitches, special shaping stitches and long stitches see the *Techniques* section on pages 122–127 of this book. Make up the finished stitching into a herb pillow as shown in the *Techniques* section.

KEY

- 321 Shading on poppy petals
- 336 Frame
- 666 Small poppy and highlights of large poppy
- 890 Dark areas on leaves
- 986 Mid-toned areas on leaves
- 988 Stems and pale areas on leaves
- 3705 Large poppy and highlights of small poppy

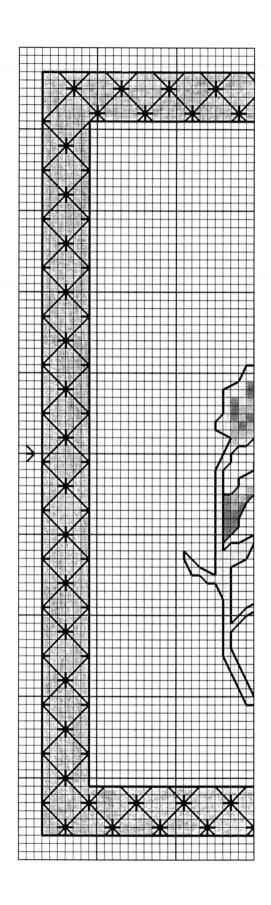

China Rose Trellis

Traditional Japanese gardens often contain some decorative trellis work. This picture, which features elements from an oriental garden, was stitched on black Aida, bringing to life the colours of the rose pink flower, the blue and yellow butterfly and the ornate golden trellis.

ACTUAL DESIGN SIZE

6¼ x 6¼in (15.5 x 15.5cm)

MATERIALS

• 1 piece of 16-count Aida in black measuring approximately 11¼ x 11¼in (28 x 28cm)
• No 24 tapestry needle

THREADS

DMC Colour	40in (1m) lengths
367 green	1
368 light green	1
470 khaki	1
472 light khaki	1
613 fawn	1
725 yellow	1
727 pale yellow	1
781 golden brown	3
800 blue	1
824 dark blue	1
890 dark green	1
891 dark pink	2
893 pink	2
894 light pink	2
937 olive green	1
3078 cream	1
3820 dark yellow	7

COLOURS FOR BACKSTITCHING

Backstitch trellis using 781.
Backstitch bamboo leaves using 937.
Backstitch flower leaves and stem using 890.
Backstitch flower petals using 891.
Backstitch butterfly body, head and antennae using 613.
Backstitch bottom edges of lower wings and eyespots on wings using 725.
Backstitch bottom part of top wings using 800.
Backstitch top part of top wings using 3820.

INSTRUCTIONS

Mark the centre of the chart. Find the centre of your fabric and make long tacking stitches across and down for guidelines. Using two strands of stranded cotton (except for backstitching where you use one strand only), begin your work following the chart. For full instructions for cross stitches, backstitches and special shaping stitches see the *Techniques* section on pages 122-127 of this book.

KEY

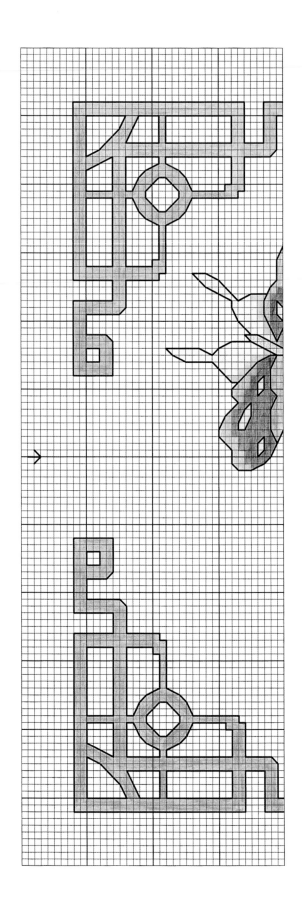

367 Stem and mid-toned areas of leaves of flower

368 Pale areas of leaves of flower

470 Dark areas of bamboo leaves

472 Pale areas of bamboo leaves

613 Butterfly's body and head

725 Dark area underneath blue butterfly wings

727 Pale area underneath blue butterfly wings

800 Pale area of butterfly wings

824 Dark area of butterfly wings

890 Dark areas of leaves and stem of flower

891 Dark centre of flower

893 Mid-toned areas of flower

894 Pale areas of flower

3078 Eyespots on butterfly wings

3820 Trellis work and top part of butterfly wings

For a lovely Mother's Day card, stitch this chrysanthemum on a slightly larger piece of fabric, then personalize it before mounting it in a card.

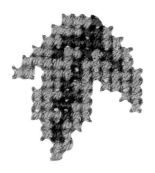

KEY

	948	Palest areas on petals
	353	Pale areas on petals
	352	Mid-toned shading on petals
	351	Darkest shading on petals
	3345	Dark shading on leaves
	3347	Mid-toned areas on leaves
	3348	Pale highlights on leaves

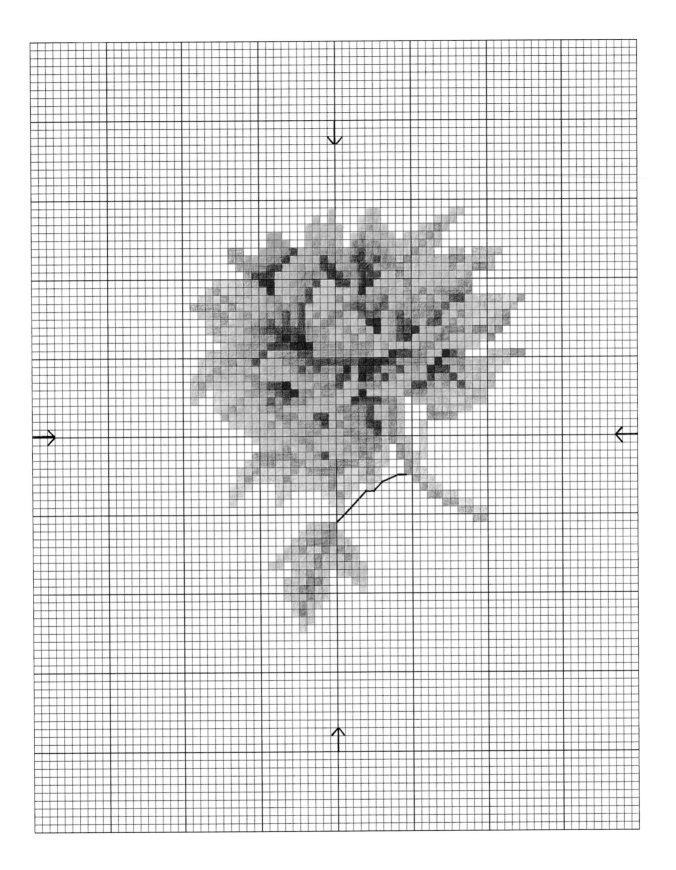

Indigo Iris

I love the intense colour of irises and wanted to create a dramatic design which would emphasize this aspect of the flower. This herb pillow is the result and it combines the beauty of the iris with the enticing scent of herbs. Another idea would be to stitch the iris on to a napkin and decorate other napkins with the remaining herb pillow designs in this book.

ACTUAL DESIGN SIZE

5¾ x 5¾in (14.5 x 14.5cm)

MATERIALS

• 1 piece of 16-count Aida in khaki measuring approximately 10¾ x 10¾in (27 x 27cm)
• No 24 tapestry needle
• 1 piece of cotton in navy measuring approximately 8¼ x 8¼in (21 x 21cm)
• Polyester filling
• Dried herbs

THREADS

DMC Colour	40in (1m) lengths
310 black	2
336 dark blue	8
726 yellow	1
797 purple	3
798 blue	2
799 light blue	2
904 green	1
3078 pale yellow	1
3821 mustard	2

COLOURS FOR BACKSTITCHING

Backstitch the trellis work on the frame using 3821.
Backstitch all other outlines using 310.

INSTRUCTIONS

Mark the centre of the chart. Find the centre of your fabric and make long tacking stitches across and down. Using two strands of stranded cotton (except for backstitching where you use one strand only), begin your work following the chart. For full instructions for cross stitches, backstitches and special shaping stitches see the *Techniques* section on pages 122-127 of this book. Make up the herb pillow following the instructions in the *Techniques* section.

KEY

▨	336	Frame
▨	726	Dark highlights of inner petals
▨	797	Dark outer edges of petals
▨	798	Mid-toned areas of petals
▨	799	Pale areas of petals
▨	904	Leaves
▨	3078	Pale highlights of inner petals

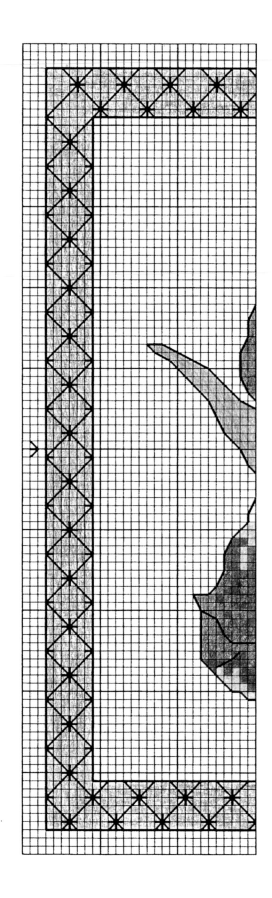

Lotus Flower

I designed this elegant lotus flower in soft shades of pink and yellow especially for a handbag mirror. As the design is so neat and compact, and so quick to stitch, you could also make it up as a gift card or even a small framed picture for a desktop.

ACTUAL DESIGN SIZE

1¾ x 2in (4.5 x 5cm)

MATERIALS

• 1 piece of 18-count Aida in cream measuring approximately 4 x 4in (10 x 10cm)
• No 24 tapestry needle
• 1 handbag mirror

INSTRUCTIONS

Mark the centre of the chart. Find the centre of your fabric and make long tacking stitches across and down. Using two strands of stranded cotton (except for backstitching where you use one strand only), begin your work following the chart. For full instructions for cross stitches, backstitches and special shaping stitches see the *Techniques* section on pages 122-127 of this book. Make up the handbag mirror following the manufacturer's instructions.

THREADS

DMC Colour	40in (1m) lengths
351 dark pink	1
352 pink	1
353 pale pink	2
746 pale yellow	1
3823 yellow	1

COLOUR FOR BACKSTITCHING

Backstitch each petal using 351.

KEY

	352	Outer edges of petals
	353	Pale areas of petals
	746	Pale areas of inner petals
	3823	Dark areas of inner petals

This quick-to-stitch picture is so pretty and delicate, it can be used in a variety of ways. You could make it into a charming ornament for a dressing table by inserting it in a trinket box, or make it into a paperweight for a desk.

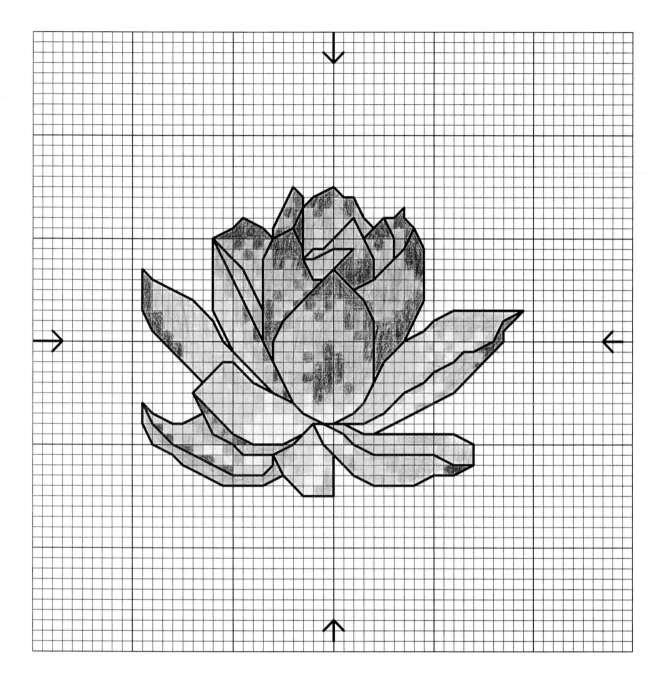

Fragile Lilies

Lilies, with their drooping flower heads and powerful scent, are one of my favourite flowers. In this design, lilies form the subject of a decorative herb pillow, framed by a trellis border. The subtle combination of cream and butter yellow make these lilies appear real.

ACTUAL DESIGN SIZE

5¾ x 5¾in (14.5 x 14.5cm)

MATERIALS

• 1 piece of 16-count Aida in khaki measuring approximately 10¾ x 10¾in (27 x 27cm)
• No 24 tapestry needle
• 1 piece of cotton in navy measuring approximately 8¼ x 8¼in (21 x 21cm)
• Polyester filling
• Herbs

THREADS

DMC Colour	40in (1m) lengths
310 black	2
336 dark blue	8
469 green	1
471 light green	3
743 dark yellow	2
744 yellow	2
746 cream	3
937 dark green	1
3821 mustard	2

INSTRUCTIONS

Mark the centre of the chart. Find the centre of your fabric and make long tacking stitches across and down. Using two strands of stranded cotton (except for backstitching where you use one strand only), begin your work following the chart. For full instructions for cross stitches, backstitches and special shaping stitches see the *Techniques* section on pages 122-127 of this book. Make up the herb pillow following the instructions in the *Techniques* section.

COLOURS FOR BACKSTITCHING

Backstitch the trellis work on the frame using 3821.
Backstitch all other outlines using 310.

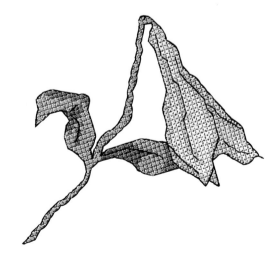

KEY

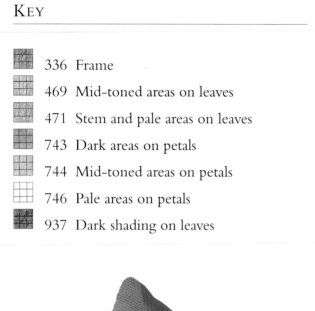

336 Frame

469 Mid-toned areas on leaves

471 Stem and pale areas on leaves

743 Dark areas on petals

744 Mid-toned areas on petals

746 Pale areas on petals

937 Dark shading on leaves

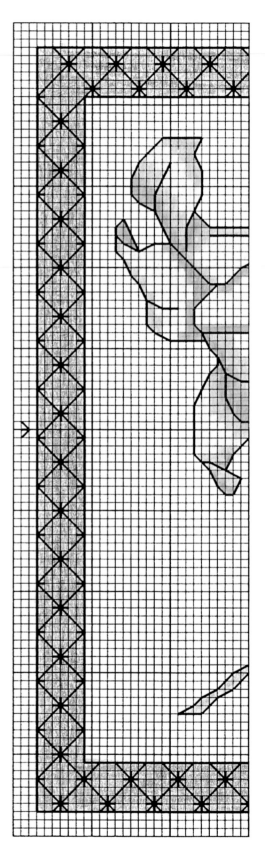

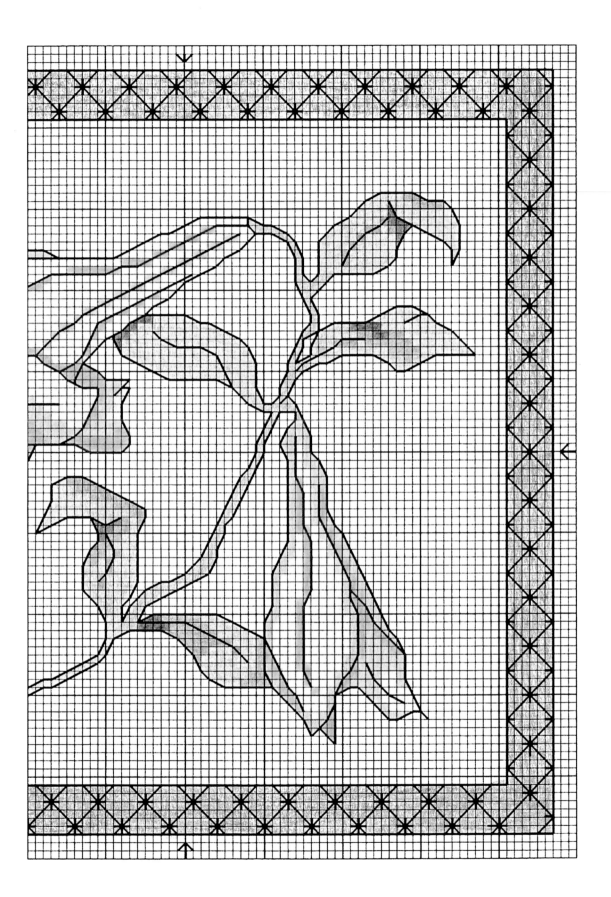

Bamboo and Flowers

This twining bamboo and flower design makes a lovely decorative border for a plain towel. Simply stitch the design on to Aida band, making it as long or as short as your towel, then sew the band to a plain guest towel. You could even decorate a set of towels in the same way.

ACTUAL DESIGN SIZE

1½ x 14in (4 x 35cm)

MATERIALS

• 1 length of 16-count Aida band in white measuring approximately 2in (5cm) wide
• No 24 tapestry needle
• 1 hand towel measuring approximately 16in (40cm) long

THREADS

DMC Colour	40in (1m) lengths
349 red	1
351 salmon pink	2
3346 dark green	1
3347 green	1
3348 light green	2

COLOURS FOR BACKSTITCHING

Backstitch the flowers using 349.
Backstitch the twining flower stems using 3346.
Backstitch the bamboo segments using 3347.

INSTRUCTIONS

Mark the centre of the chart. Find the centre of your fabric and make long tacking stitches across and down. Using two strands of stranded cotton (except for backstitching where you use one strand only), begin your work following the chart. For full instructions for cross stitches, backstitches and special shaping stitches see the *Techniques* section on pages 122-127 of this book. Slipstitch the Aida band on to a guest towel to complete.

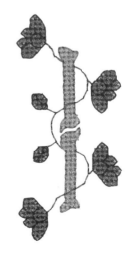

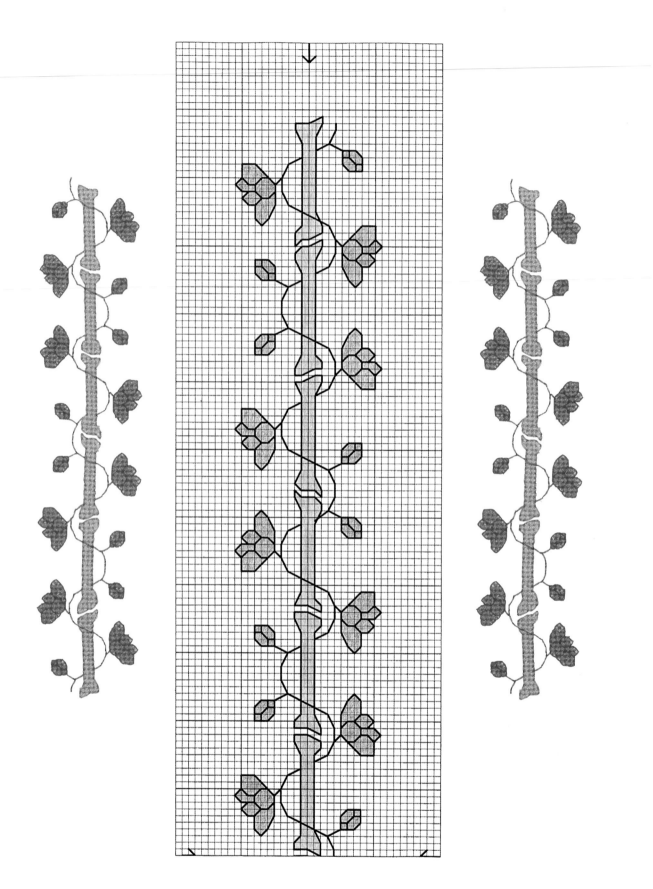

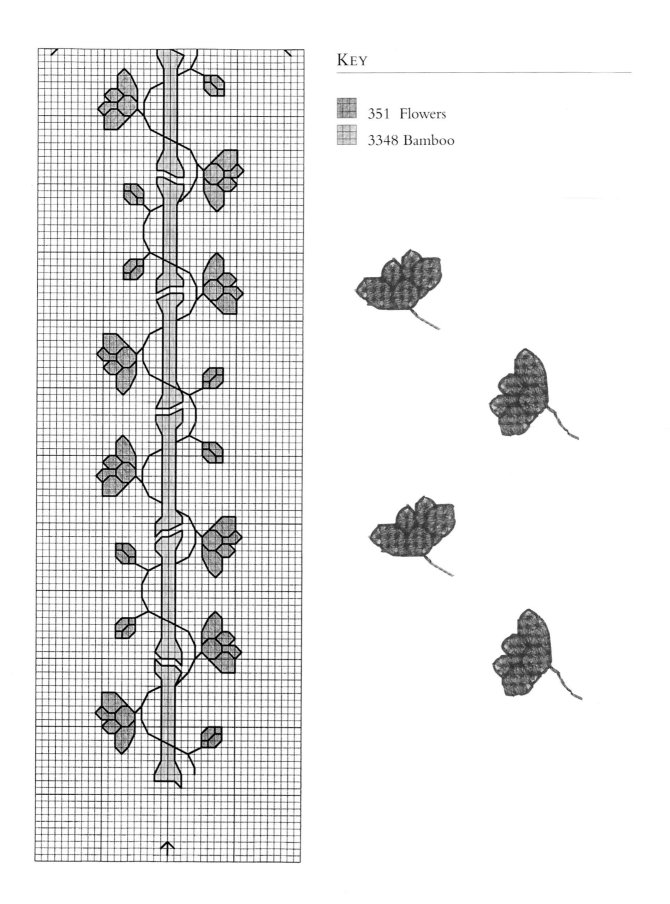

KEY

351 Flowers
3348 Bamboo

Floral Fans

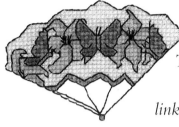

This stylish bookmark depicts three open fans, each illustrating an oriental stylized design of flowers, birds and butterflies. The delicate colours, linked by the background colour of pale yellow, combine to create a subtle and elegant bookmark.

ACTUAL DESIGN SIZE

6¾ x 2in (17 x 5cm)

MATERIALS

• 1 piece of 36-count Linen in ivory measuring approximately 11½ x 6¾in (29 x 17cm)
• No 24 tapestry needle
• 1 piece of lace measuring approximately 40in (1m) (optional)
• 1 piece of ribbon measuring approximately 10in (25cm) (optional)
• 3 ribbon bows (optional)

THREADS

DMC Colour	40in (1m) lengths
208 purple	1
209 light purple	1
310 black	1
319 green	1
436 brown	1
746 cream	1
823 dark blue	1
922 terracotta	1
3755 blue	1
3820 light brown	1
3822 yellow	1

COLOUR FOR BACKSTITCHING

Backstitch all outlines using 310.

INSTRUCTIONS

Mark the centre of the chart. Find the centre of your fabric and make tacking stitches across and down. Using two strands of stranded cotton (except for backstitching where you use one strand only), begin your work following the chart. For details of stitches see the *Techniques* section on pages 122-127. Make up the bookmark following the instructions in the *Techniques* section.

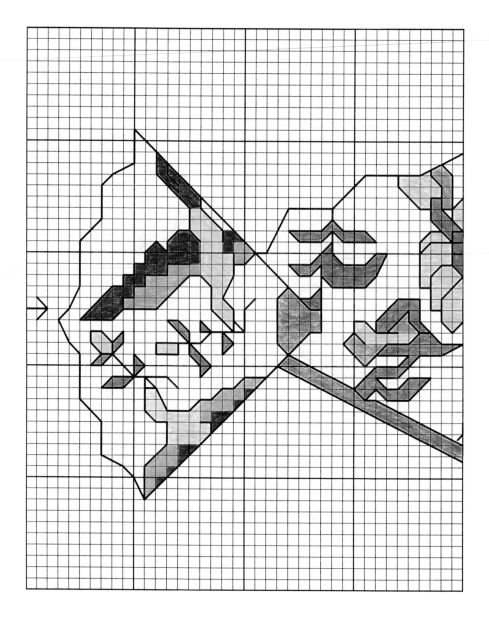

KEY

208 Dark areas on butterfly wings

209 Light areas on butterfly wings

319 Stems and leaves

436 Handles of two right fans and lower edge of left fan

746 Background of fans

823 Dark areas of birds' wings

922 Centre of large flower

3755 Pale areas of birds' wings

3820 Dark areas of flower petals

3822 Light areas of flower petals

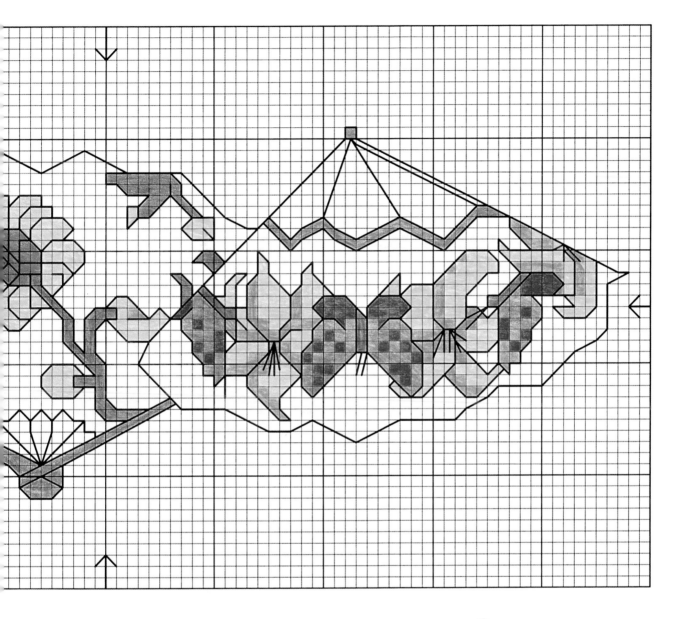

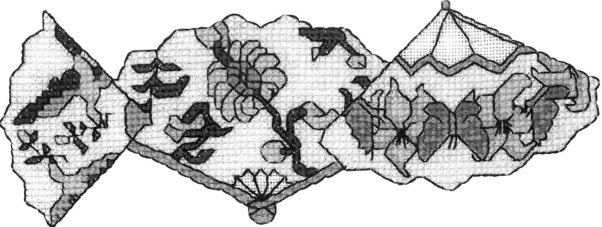

Exquisite Bonsai

I find bonsai trees fascinating because they are so tiny and yet so perfect. I stitched four different miniature bonsai designs to illustrate the diversity of shapes and colours they can create. These designs were stitched for gift cards but you could frame them to make a set of pictures if you prefer.

YELLOW-POTTED BONSAI

ACTUAL DESIGN SIZE

3 x 2½in (7.5 x 6.5cm)

MATERIALS

- 1 piece of 36-count Linen in ivory measuring approximately 7¾ x 7⅜in (19.5 x 18.5cm)
- No 24 tapestry needle
- Gift card (optional)

THREADS

DMC Colour	40in (1m) lengths
433 brown	1
783 butterscotch	1
801 dark brown	1
938 chocolate brown	1
986 dark forest green	1
987 forest green	1
988 light forest green	1
3371 dark chocolate brown	1
3820 light butterscotch	1
3822 yellow	1
3823 pale yellow	1

COLOURS FOR BACKSTITCHING

Backstitch detail on pot using 783.
Backstitch branch using 801.
Backstitch soil using 3371.

INSTRUCTIONS

Mark the centre of the chart. Find the centre of your fabric and make long tacking stitches across and down. Using two strands of stranded cotton (except for backstitching where you use one strand only), begin your work following the chart. For full instructions for cross stitches, backstitches and special shaping stitches see the *Techniques* section on pages 122–127 of this book.

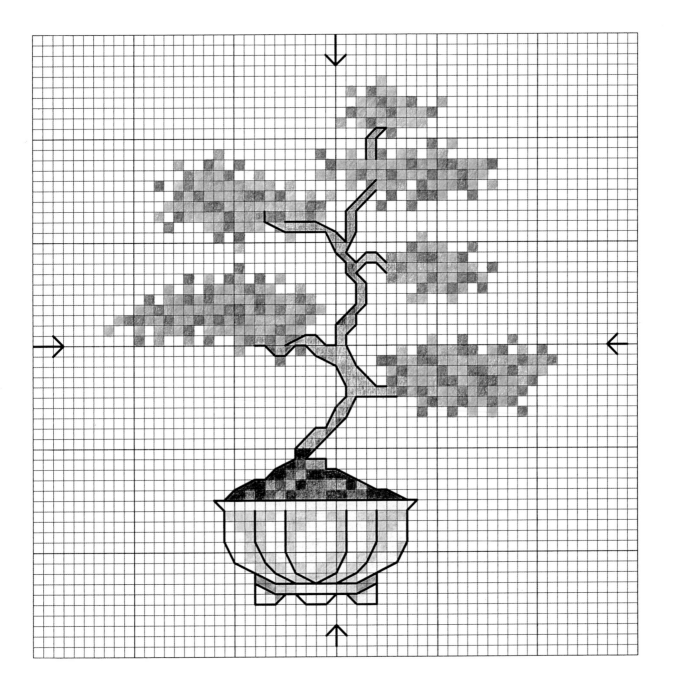

KEY

433 Light areas of branch

801 Soil and shading on branch

938 Soil

986 Dark leaves

987 Mid-toned leaves

988 Pale leaves

3371 Dark areas of soil

3820 Base of pot

3822 Shading on pot

3823 Pot rim and pale areas of pot

GREEN-POTTED BONSAI

ACTUAL DESIGN SIZE

3½ x 3½in (9 x 9cm)

MATERIALS

• 1 piece of 36-count Linen in ivory measuring approximately 8½ x 8½in (21 x 21cm)
• No 24 tapestry needle
• Gift card (optional)

THREADS

DMC Colour	40in (1m) lengths
433 brown	1
435 caramel	1
437 light caramel	1
469 olive	1
471 light olive	1
500 dark pine green	2
501 pine green	3
503 light pine green	2
801 dark brown	1
839 light brown	1
934 dark olive	1
937 sage green	1

COLOURS FOR BACKSTITCHING

Backstitch the branch and trunk using 433.
Backstitch the pot using 934.

INSTRUCTIONS

Mark the centre of the chart. Find the centre of your fabric and make long tacking stitches across and down for guidelines. Using two strands of stranded cotton (except for backstitching where you use one strand only),

begin your work following the chart. For full instructions for cross stitches, backstitches and special shaping stitches see the *Techniques* section on pages 122-127 of this book.

KEY

433 Trunk and branches
435 Dark areas of trunk and branches
437 Pale areas of trunk and branches
469 Mid-toned areas of pot
471 Centre of pot
500 Dark leaves
501 Mid-toned leaves
503 Pale leaves
801 Dark areas of trunk and top branches
839 Soil
937 Outer edges of pot

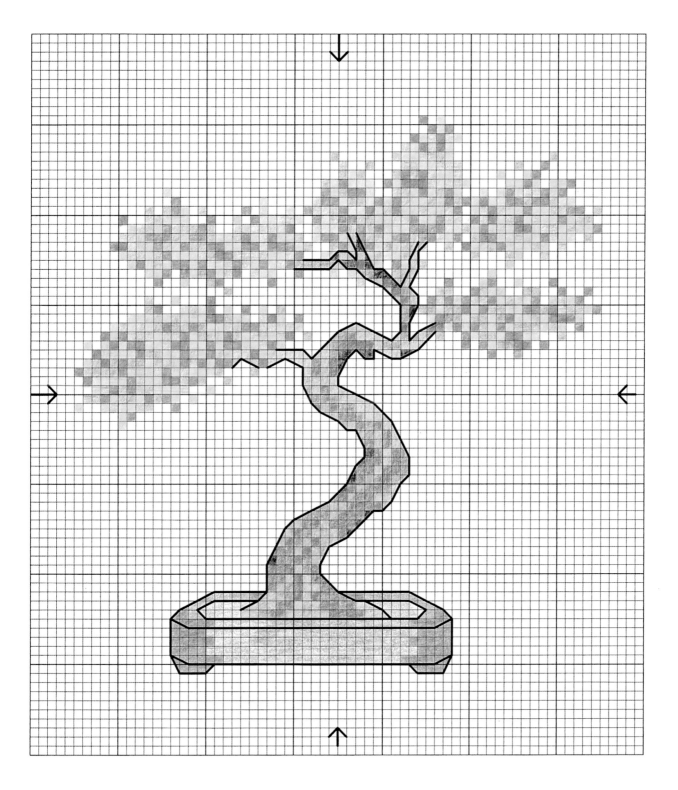

RED-POTTED BONSAI

ACTUAL DESIGN SIZE

2½ x 3in (6.5 x 7.5cm)

MATERIALS

• 1 piece of 36-count Linen in ivory measuring approximately 7½ x 8in (19 x 20cm)
• No 24 tapestry needle
• Gift card (optional)

INSTRUCTIONS

Mark the centre of the chart. Find the centre of your fabric and make long tacking stitches across and down. Using two strands of stranded cotton (except for backstitching where you use one strand only), begin your work following the chart. For full instructions for cross stitches, backstitches and special shaping stitches see the *Techniques* section on pages 122-127.

THREADS

DMC Colour	40in (1m) lengths
350 red	1
351 dark pink	1
352 pink	1
353 light pink	1
838 dark brown	1
839 brown	1
840 light brown	1
904 dark green	2
905 green	2
907 light green	2
948 pale pink	1

COLOURS FOR BACKSTITCHING

Backstitch the pot using 350.
Backstitch the trunk and branches using 838.

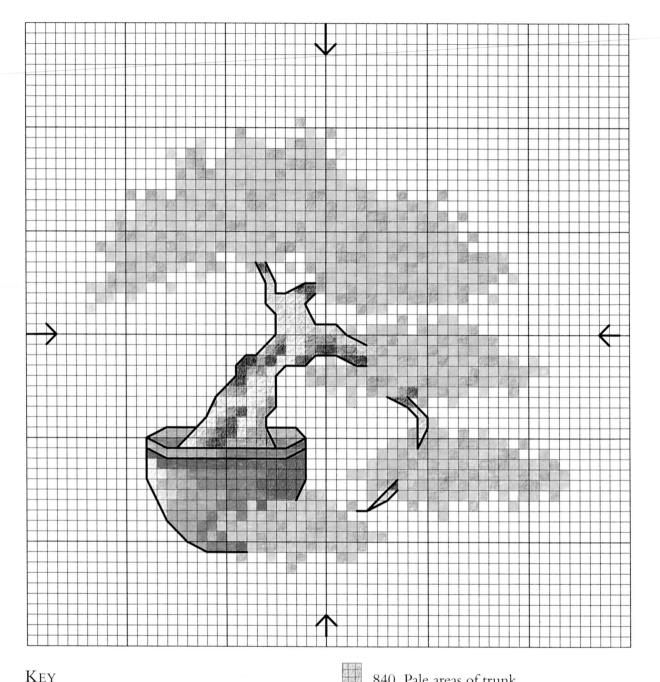

KEY

	351 Dark side of pot, on the right
	352 Centre of the pot
	353 Light side of pot, on the left
	838 Dark areas of trunk and branches
	839 Mid-toned trunk and branches

840 Pale areas of trunk

904 Dark leaves

905 Mid-toned leaves

907 Light leaves

948 Highlights of pot, on the left

BLUE-POTTED BONSAI

ACTUAL DESIGN SIZE

4 x 2½in (10 x 8cm)

MATERIALS

- 1 piece of 36-count Linen in ivory measuring approximately 8½ x 8½in (21 x 21cm)
- No 24 tapestry needle
- Gift card (optional)

THREADS

DMC Colour	40in (1m) lengths
312 dark blue	1
322 blue	1
334 light blue	1
801 brown	1
934 dark olive green	2
936 olive green	2
938 chocolate brown	1
3346 dark green	2
3347 green	2
3348 light green	2
3371 dark chocolate brown	1
3755 light blue	1

COLOURS FOR BACKSTITCHING

Backstitch the pot using 312.
Backstitch the trunk and branches using 3371.

INSTRUCTIONS

Mark the centre of the chart. Find the centre of your fabric and make long tacking stitches across and down. Using two strands of stranded cotton (except for backstitching where you use one strand only), begin your work following the chart. For full instructions for cross stitches, backstitches and special shaping stitches see the *Techniques* section on pages 122-127 of this book.

KEY

322	Outer edges of pot	
334	Mid-toned areas of pot	
801	Dark areas of trunk	
934	Dark-coloured moss at base of trunk	
936	Pale-coloured moss at base of trunk	
938	Lower half of trunk	
3346	Dark leaves	

3347 Mid-toned leaves

3348 Pale leaves

3371 Lower half of trunk

3755 Centre section of pot

Techniques

This section introduces the basic materials you need for cross stitch, and the skills you need to master – including stitching, finishing and framing – to be able to begin stitching the cross-stitch projects in this book.

TIPS

◆ Always work with clean hands.
◆ Do not drag threads across spaces where there are no cross stitches, this will show up when the piece is stretched.
◆ Let the needle hang regularly to avoid twisting the thread.
◆ Take the work out of the embroidery hoop at night or when you stop working to avoid marking the fabric.
◆ Attach your needle to the extreme outer edge of the fabric while you are not stitching. This avoids marking the fabric.

MATERIALS

You will need to stitch on an evenweave fabric which is a fabric that has the same number of weft (horizontal) threads as it has warp (vertical) threads.

LINEN

This is a natural fibre so the thickness of the threads may vary across the fabric. Linen is also more expensive than Aida but as you stitch over two threads, it is much easier to use when you are stitching quarter, three-quarter and special shaping stitches. Stitching on linen produces an irregular effect.

A full cross stitch worked over two threads on linen.

AIDA

Beginners may find it easier to stitch on Aida fabric. The threads are woven in blocks which makes them easier to count and your stitches will look more even. You generally stitch over one block.

A full cross stitch worked over one block on Aida.

WASTE CANVAS

This versatile material enables you to stitch a design on to almost anything – pillowslips, T-shirts, jumpers. Baste the waste canvas on to your chosen item and then stitch your design as normal. When you've finished, unpick the basting stitches. Gently dampen your work and pull out the waste canvas with tweezers. If you pull out the vertical threads first, the horizontal threads will then be easier to remove.

Design Size

It is important to know the 'count' of fabric you choose, as this will determine the finished size of your design. The finer the fabric, the smaller the stitches eg '18-count' Aida means there are 18 blocks to the inch, therefore producing 18 stitches to the inch. If you use '14-count' Aida your finished design will be larger as you are stitching with 14 squares to the inch. When you work on linen you stitch over two threads, so if you stitch on 32-count linen you will have 16 stitches to the inch.

Always remember to allow about 2½in (6.5cm) on each side of the design for stretching and framing.

Threads

I have used DMC threads in my designs as the choice of colours is superb and the quality is beautiful. There are also other brands of thread available that you can use. However, the colours of other brands may not match the DMC colours exactly so the finished piece may have a different character.

Stranded Cotton (Floss)

This is made up of six strands of mercerized cotton that can be separated into single strands or groups of two or more. Most of the designs in this book are worked with two strands for cross stitches and one strand for backstitching. If you prefer a softer image, use one strand for cross stitches. Always pull one strand out at a time then put the two strands together.

Perle Cotton

This is a mercerized thread that is non-divisible and has a soft gloss when stitched.

Flower Thread

This is a non-divisible matt yarn designed mainly for work on fine fabrics eg linen.

Be Organized

A thread organizer is invaluable. It is a piece of card with holes punched down each side. You can easily make one yourself. Once you have chosen the colours you need, cut them into 20in (50cm) or 40in (1m) lengths and thread them through the holes of the thread organizer. Label them with the colour number and when you need to use one length of thread you just remove the thread from the organizer, take off the required number of strands and replace the rest back in the thread organizer.

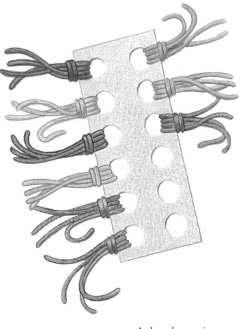

A thread organizer

FRAMES

It is personal preference whether or not you use a frame or embroidery hoop. It depends a lot on your stitching tension but as a rule, using an embroidery hoop makes stitching easier. It keeps your fabric taut and does not let it stretch and distort.

NEEDLES

For all counted needlework you will need a blunt tapestry needle. I use a size 24 tapestry needle as it is very comfortable to hold without being too thin or too chunky. For working on waste canvas you will need a crewel needle, which has a sharp point and flat eye enabling several strands to be used at once, or as required.

CHARTS

Each colour on the chart represents a colour of thread. Each square of colour represents one cross stitch. The backstitching is identified by solid lines. You will probably find it easier working in blocks of colour than rows. You will also find it helpful to have a few needles threaded with different colours, so when you change to a different colour you are ready to stitch right away.

LET'S BEGIN!

The first thing to do is find the centre of the fabric. To do this fold your fabric in half both ways. The centre is the best place to begin stitching, as your work will then be correctly positioned on the fabric. You can put long tacking stitches across and down to mark the centre to act as guidelines. Remove these when you have started your work.

All your underneath stitches must run in the same direction, so that all your top stitches will also be going the same way. Don't stitch one cross at a time unless it is a single cross stitch in a different colour to the surrounding stitches. Stitch in a row – if you have 10 cross stitches to work, stitch the 10 underneath stitches first then turn back on yourself and complete the crosses.

STARTING AND FINISHING

STARTING

Try not to use knots, as these look very unsightly when the design is finished and stretched. Anchor your thread in place by bringing your needle up through the back of the fabric where you are ready to start. Leave a tail long enough to be caught by your next few stitches and then trim the end. Look at the back of your work to check that the tail has been secured after the first few stitches.

FINISHING OFF

To finish off without using a knot, weave the thread through the backs of four or five adjacent stitches and trim the end.

CROSS STITCHES EXPLAINED

FULL CROSS STITCHES ON AIDA

To make one cross stitch, think of the stitch area as a square of four holes. Bring the needle up through the hole in the bottom left corner of the square and then down through the hole in the top right corner. Then take the needle up through the bottom right hole and down into the top left hole.

To stitch a row of cross stitches in the same colour, bring your needle up at the bottom left hole and down in the top right hole. Do not finish the stitch but continue this step until you complete the correct number of stitches going one way. Then work back along the row to complete your cross stitches ie from bottom right to top left. Stitching in this way ensures that the line is even and regular.

FULL CROSS STITCHES ON LINEN

To stitch a single cross stitch on linen, follow the instructions as for cross stitching on Aida, but stitch across two threads of the fabric.

QUARTER STITCHES

These are indicated by a colour in a corner of a square. Work a quarter stitch as shown below. If you are using Aida, you will have to split the centre threads on the Aida with your needle. You will often find two quarter stitches in the

Quarter stitch

same block but using different colours. This is stitched very simply by stitching your first quarter stitch in one colour then, when you work your second quarter stitch in the second colour, push your needle into the same hole in the centre of the block.

If you stitch backstitches over the top after you have finished all your cross stitching, this will hide any spaces.

HALF-CROSS STITCHES

A half-cross stitch is half of a full cross stitch – in other words a diagonal stitch. It is usually used as shading in the designs in this book.

THREE-QUARTER STITCHES

I have used these stitches primarily with the special shaping stitches (described below). Work a quarter stitch as described earlier and then make a diagonal half stitch across it.

Three-quarter stitch

SPECIAL SHAPING STITCHES

I created this stitch to give gentle sloping lines in and around the edge of the designs. It is stitched over two blocks. This is indicated on the charts by three-quarters of a square being in a colour and a quarter of the next square being in the same colour. Therefore you stitch a three-quarter stitch and a quarter stitch (see the illustration below). Your backstitching over the top will complete the design, shown below by a dotted line.

Special shaping stitch

BACKSTITCHING

Backstitching is shown by a continuous line and should be worked after the design has been completed. When the chart shows a backstitch across a cross stitch, the backstitch should be worked on the top of the stitch.

FRENCH KNOTS

This will be indicated on the chart by a dot. To stitch, bring the needle up where you want the knot to be. Hold the thread as it comes out of the fabric and place the needle behind it. Twist the needle twice around the thread and insert the needle back into the fabric slightly away from where you started, keeping the thread taut all the time. Practise this on a spare piece of fabric before stitching on your work.

French knot

LONG STITCHES

Long stitches are quite literally long stitches – where they are shown on the charts, just stitch that whole length with one stitch.

FINISHING

LOOKING AFTER YOUR FABRIC

It is inevitable that your work will require washing after being completed. The threads are meant to be colourfast, but to be on the safe side, take great care when washing. Immerse your work in lukewarm soapy water and gently wash by hand. Do not rub vigorously. Dry flat face down on a towel and iron on the reverse side to prevent the stitches being flattened.

LACING

Cut a piece of acid-free mount board to the same size as the inside of your frame. Centre your work on the board and insert pins along the top edge. Use the fabric holes to help you keep the edges straight. Gently pull the fabric and pin along the bottom edge in the same way. Repeat with the sides. Turn your project over and with a large-eyed needle and crochet cotton (which must be knotted) lace the fabric from top to bottom using an under-and-over movement, ensuring that the fabric is taut. Then repeat from side to side. Stitch the corners down and remove the pins – you can now frame your work.

FRAMING

MOUNTING INTO GIFT CARDS

The cards used in this book have been mounted in 3-fold cards. A wide variety of cards are

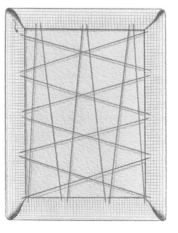

Lacing

available in needlework or craft shops. Follow the individual manufacturer's instructions for mounting your work.

MOUNTING ON TO FLEXI-HOOPS

Centre your design in the flexi-hoop and place in the flexi-hoop. Trim the spare fabric on the back to 1in (2.5cm). I usually put some wadding in the middle to give some density to the picture. Lace the ends across the back of the flexi-hoop and then glue a piece of felt over them for a neat finish.

MAKING A BOOKMARK

Making sure the stitched design is central, trim the excess fabric from around the stitching so that the bookmark measures 2½ x 7in (6.5 x 17.5cm). Neaten the edges by sewing by machine or by hand. Pin a length of lace around the bookmark, starting and finishing at the bottom edge. Mitre the lace at the corners, then stitch the lace in place. Stitch trimmings of your choice, for example, ribbons, tassels or bows, to the bottom of the bookmark, covering the join in the lace.

MAKING A HERB PILLOW

Making sure the stitched design is central, trim the Aida to 1½in (4cm) all round the edge of design. Trim a backing cloth to the same dimensions as the Aida. Place the Aida and backing cloth right sides together and stitch around three sides ⅝in (1.5cm) from the edge. Turn the pillow the right way out and stuff with polyester filling and dried herbs. Finally, slipstitch the unstitched side to close and plump up the pillow to complete.

Acknowledgements

I would like to thank:

My wonderful husband Graham, my three children, Danielle, David and Richard, and my Mum. Their support is endless and unconditional.

Jane Prutton, my designer at Designer Stitches UK Ltd, who assisted me throughout the book. Jane's coloured charts are beautiful and I could not have finished the book in time without her.

Helena Mottershead, my Head of Design, at Designer Stitches UK Ltd.

Jackie Hrycan for the charting of the designs.

Danielle, my daughter, for stitching and checking thread counts.

All my loyal staff at Designer Stitches UK Ltd, who helped me in every capacity.

And, of course, all my beautiful stitchers all over the country, who pulled out all the stops.

I would also like to thank the following companies for the supplies used in this book:

Framecraft Miniatures for their trinket boxes and handbag mirror.

DMC for their threads.

All the Aida and Linen used in this book has been supplied by my own company, Designer Stitches UK Ltd, using 'Debbie Minton's Designer Fabrics'.

These are available from:

Designer Stitches UK Ltd
Earl Road
Cheadle Hulme
Cheshire SK8 6PQ
UK
Tel: +44 (0)161 482 6200
Fax: +44 (0)161 482 8000
Email: sales@designerstitches.co.uk

'Debbie Minton's Designer Fabrics' are available in many shades and sizes, and are distributed worldwide.